WORLD
HISTORY SERIES

The Crash
of 1929

Titles in the World History Series

WORLD HISTORY SERIES ▪▪▪

The Crash of 1929

by
Nathan Aaseng

Lucent Books, P.O. Box 289011, San Diego, CA 92198-9011

On Cover: The New York Stock Exchange
New York, N.Y., 1929.

Library of Congress Cataloging-in-Publication Data

Aaseng, Nathan.
  The Crash of 1929 / by Nathan Aaseng.
    p. cm.—(World history series)
Includes bibliographical references and index.
  ISBN 1-56006-804-3 (alk. paper)
 1. Stock Market Crash, 1929—Juvenile literature. 2. United
States—Economic conditions—1918–1945—Juvenile literature.
[1. Stock Market Crash, 1929. 2. United States—Economic
conditions—1918–1945. 3. Depressions—1929.] I. Title. II. Series.
  HB3717 1929 .A2 2001
  338.5'4'097309043—dc21

                                              00-012613

Copyright 2001 by Lucent Books, Inc., P.O. Box 289011,
San Diego, California 92198-9011

Printed in the U.S.A.

Contents

Foreword

Each year on the first day of school, nearly every history teacher faces the task of explaining why his or her students should study history. One logical answer to this question is that exploring what happened in our past explains how the things we often take for granted—our customs, ideas, and institutions—came to be. As statesman and historian Winston Churchill put it, "Every nation or group of nations has its own tale to tell. Knowledge of the trials and struggles is necessary to all who would comprehend the problems, perils, challenges, and opportunities which confront us today." Thus, a study of history puts modern ideas and institutions in perspective. For example, though the founders of the United States were talented and creative thinkers, they clearly did not invent the concept of democracy. Instead, they adapted some democratic ideas that had originated in ancient Greece and with which the Romans, the British, and others had experimented. An exploration of these cultures, then, reveals their very real connection to us through institutions that continue to shape our daily lives.

Another reason often given for studying history is the idea that lessons exist in the past from which contemporary societies can benefit and learn. This idea, although controversial, has always been an intriguing one for historians. Those who agree that society can benefit from the past often quote philosopher George Santayana's famous statement, "Those who cannot remember the past are condemned to repeat it." Historians who subscribe to Santayana's philosophy believe that, for example, studying the events that led up to the major world wars or other significant historical events would allow society to chart a different and more favorable course in the future.

Just as difficult as convincing students to realize the importance of studying history is the search for useful and interesting supplementary materials that present historical events in a context that can be easily understood. The volumes in Lucent Books' World History Series attempt to present a broad, balanced, and penetrating view of the march of history. Ancient Egypt's important wars and rulers, for example, are presented against the rich and colorful backdrop of Egyptian religious, social, and cultural developments. The series engages the reader by enhancing historical events with these cultural contexts. For example, in *Ancient Greece*, the text covers the role of women in that society. Slavery is discussed in *The Roman Empire*, as well as how slaves earned their freedom. The numerous and varied aspects of everyday life in these and other societies are explored in each volume of the series. Additionally, the series covers the major political, cultural, and philosophical ideas as the torch of civilization is passed from ancient Mesopotamia and Egypt, through Greece, Rome, Medieval Europe, and other world cultures, to the modern day.

The material in the series is formatted in a thorough, precise, and organized manner. Each volume offers the reader a comprehensive and clearly written overview of an important historical event or period. The topic under discussion is placed in a broad, historical context. For example, *The Italian Renaissance* begins with a discussion of the High Middle Ages and the loss of central control that allowed certain Italian cities to develop artistically. The book ends by looking forward to the Reformation and interpreting the societal changes that grew out of the Renaissance. Thus, students are not only involved in an historical era, but also enveloped by the events leading up to that era and the events following it.

One important and unique feature in the World History Series is the primary and secondary source quotations that richly supplement each volume. These quotes are useful in a number of ways. First, they allow students access to sources they would not normally be exposed to because of the difficulty and obscurity of the original source. The quotations range from interesting anecdotes to farsighted cultural perspectives and are drawn from historical witnesses both past and present. Second, the quotes demonstrate how and where historians themselves derive their information on the past as they strive to reach a consensus on historical events. Lastly, all of the quotes are footnoted, familiarizing students with the citation process and allowing them to verify quotes and/or look up the original source if the quote piques their interest.

Finally, the books in the World History Series provide a detailed launching point for further research. Each book contains a bibliography specifically geared toward student research. A second, annotated bibliography introduces students to all the sources the author consulted when compiling the book. A chronology of important dates gives students an overview, at a glance, of the topic covered. Where applicable, a glossary of terms is included.

In short, the series is designed not only to acquaint readers with the basics of history, but also to make them aware that their lives are a part of an ongoing human saga. Perhaps they will then come to the same realization as famed historian Arnold Toynbee. In his monumental work, *A Study of History*, he wrote about becoming aware of history flowing through him in a mighty current, and of his own life "welling like a wave in the flow of this vast tide."

What a Country! What a Time To Be Alive!

William C. Durant was not alone in thinking these thoughts as he enjoyed his Labor Day weekend in September 1929. World War I, the terrible "war to end all wars" as politicians termed it, was now only a fading memory. The United States had used the emergency war production as a springboard to mount the greatest economic boom in the history of the world. Along with millions of Americans, Durant had discovered that the riches of the stock market were as profitable as a gold mine and far easier to obtain. And no one played the stock market with more daring and skill than Billy Durant.

The Boston-born Durant was a classic example of the American Dream. He was born during the horrors of the Civil War in 1861 and his father deserted him at a young age. With determination and skill, he rose up from his humble beginnings to launch a career as a self-made businessman. At the age of twenty-five, he took over a small carriage-making company in Flint, Michigan, and built it into one of the most prosperous firms in the city.

In 1904 he bought out the floundering Buick Motor Company at a time when cutthroat competition was driving most automakers into bankruptcy. Through a series of shrewd and aggressive financial maneuvers he acquired other struggling companies and so added the Oldsmobile, Cadillac, and Pontiac divisions to his reorganized General Motors business. Durant even came within an eyelash of adding the legendary rival Ford Motor Company to his empire. But even though that sale fell through, Durant's expert promotion and management set General Motors on the path to becoming the largest corporation in the world.

A huge-stakes gambler like Durant occasionally suffered losses that were as spectacular as his successes in the car business. He took on such an enormous debt in his rapid expansion of General Motors that in 1910 he had to surrender control of the company to investors. Undaunted, he started a new company, Chevrolet, and it became such a great success that he used its profits to regain control of General Motors.

Then in 1920 his ambitious plans for further expansion plunged him back into debt and he was forced out of the auto business.

During all of his wheeling and dealing, Durant had developed a flair for creative investing in the stock market. Making use of the many contacts he had made as head of General Motors, he gathered investors willing to follow his lead in buying and selling stocks on the New York Stock Exchange. From 1924 to 1929, Durant and his syndicate poured an estimated $4 billion into selected stocks. Knowing the reputation that Durant and his friends had for making shrewd investments, millions of Americans followed Durant's lead and used their savings to buy these same stocks. The increased demand for these stocks, along with the generally booming United States economy, earned breathtaking profits for Durant and his syndicate. According to many stock market observers, Durant made more money on the stock market than any other person in the 1920s. Once he

General Motors founder William C. Durant made shrewd, daring, and highly profitable stock market investments in the 1920s.

raked in an estimated $50 million in just three months, and he accumulated a total profit believed to be over $100 million.

Not only Durant, but millions of small investors sailed along on this wave of prosperity, making more money than they had imagined possible. With Herbert Hoover, widely regarded as the most brilliant and able public figure of the generation, taking over as president of the United States, that prosperity promised to stretch far out into the foreseeable future.

Within two months of that joyous Labor Day, however, the bottom dropped out of that comfortable world. Millions of Ameri-cans watched in horror as their life savings vanished before their eyes. Will Durant not only lost his entire fortune but, by the time he emerged from the wreckage of the stock market crash, fell so deeply in debt that he eventually had to declare bankruptcy. The shock of the financial catastrophe threw the nation into the worst economic depression of its history—a depression that destroyed lives, families, and changed the face of United States culture forever.

In just two traumatic days, millions of dreams were shattered. Durant and the legions of ordinary investors never saw it coming.

1 The Roaring Twenties

The 1920s was a decade of change and excitement throughout most of the Western world. The terrible world war had scrambled the boundaries of Europe, giving landlocked Poland a corridor to the sea and granting independence to people in small countries such as Austria, Hungary, Yugoslavia, Czechoslovakia, Estonia, Latvia, and Lithuania. The United States opened the decade by venturing into two daring social experiments: Prohibition, which outlawed the sale of alcoholic beverages, and granting increased rights to women. Not only did American women gain the right to vote in 1920, but society had begun to accept the presence of women in the workplace, in institutions of higher learning, and in professional fields.

U.S. INDUSTRIAL EXPANSION

But the major cause for excitement was the unprecedented economic explosion taking place in the United States. The dire consequences of war had forced the United States to expand and modernize those industries that contributed most to the war effort, such as iron, steel, oil, and chemical plants. When the war ended, the enormous production from these factories was turned loose on American consumers.

Other manufacturers quickly followed the innovative lead of the war production industries in streamlining production, expanding facilities, and increasing efficiency by replacing human labor with machines. U.S. industry nearly doubled its production

The U.S. steel industry experienced tremendous growth and modernization during World War I.

between 1919 and 1929. Construction of power plants rose by 15 percent a year for the entire decade. In a single year, 1923, the nation's gross national product (the measure of all the goods and services produced in the country) rose an astonishing 14 percent.

At the same time, inflation (the increase in prices over time) was virtually nonexistent. Unemployment was generally low, as even modernized factories needed many workers to keep up with increased production demands. The combined effect of these economic conditions was that the United States basked in one of the most prosperous times in history. The nation shot far ahead of the rest of the world in the accumulation of wealth. By the late 1920s the United States had gained control of roughly 40 percent of the world's riches. Its national income was greater than the next wealthiest countries in the world— Great Britain, France, Italy, Germany, and Japan—combined, *plus* the combined income of the next dozen wealthiest nations. The United States was producing so much that its trade surplus topped $1 billion, meaning that it sold $1 billion more in goods to other nations than it bought from them.

The good times showed no signs of fading as the decade wound down. In 1929, figures were released showing that United States steel mills had enjoyed another record year of production in 1928. U.S. Steel then topped that by announcing that it had earned record peacetime profits for the first half of 1929. General Motors also reported the highest earnings in its history.

NEW ERA OF BIG BUSINESS

With American industries churning out so many goods and services, competition to gain buyers for these goods and services grew fierce. In most cases it was a matter of survival of the fittest. Large, stable, well-financed companies invested heavily in expansion. Before long, they drove out or absorbed their smaller competitors and, in the process, grew even larger. Firms that had trouble competing often opted to merge with other companies in order to gain the resources to challenge their larger competitors. Many small companies simply went out of business.

Mass production proved enormously profitable for big companies. Near the end of the 1920s, annual corporate profits skyrocketed an average of 63 percent a year. Profits of financial institutions rose an incredible 150 percent. Flush with these profits, large corporations so dominated the nation's economy that by the end of the decade a mere two hundred companies were responsible for half of the nation's corporate wealth.

The automobile industry served as a prime example of the new era of big business. Dozens of small automakers closed their doors, unable to compete with the growing financial muscle of the Ford Motor Company, whose revolutionary assembly line allowed it to make eight thousand cars a day. Will Durant survived only by folding many car manufacturers into one large corporation, General Motors. In 1929, two smaller but reputable companies, Chrysler and Dodge, had to merge in order to stay competitive. These three giants—Ford,

Mass production at the Ford Motor Company, whose assembly line could turn out 8,000 cars per day in 1929, drove many smaller automakers out of business.

General Motors, and Chrysler—quickly overwhelmed their smaller competitors. By the end of the decade the Big Three produced more than eight of every ten automobiles manufactured in the country.

The story was repeated in other industries such as steel, where U.S. Steel ruled the roost, and telecommunications, where AT&T dominated. In the decade of the twenties, three companies handled the vast majority of the nation's life insurance policies. One percent of the nation's thirty thousand banks controlled 40 percent of the monetary assets. A single grocery chain, A&P, captured one-tenth of all the retail food business in the nation.

Size was so important to survival that businesses became obsessed with bigness. They pumped millions of dollars into new factories and expanded production capacity. The result was a drastic change in the distribution of products. Formerly, consumers were limited to a small supply of relatively expensive products made or delivered by businesspeople they knew personally. The era of big business brought in great supplies of products that could be made and sold more cheaply. The tradeoff was that consumers and employees had to do business with large, faceless, impersonal corporations rather than people.

INDIVIDUAL PROSPERITY

This booming economy delivered by big business meant that Americans had far more money available for purchasing needs and wants than previous generations. The average income of Americans rose nearly 20 percent during the decade. Again, the most glaring example of this newfound consumer purchasing power was the automobile. Middle-class Americans lined up to purchase what only a decade before had been considered a luxury for the rich. In order to meet the demand for cars, United States factories were cranking out over four million automobiles a year. The rest of the world combined made fewer than one million.

Everywhere one looked, evidence of the great abundance brought about by America's factories was visible. The number of millionaires in the nation jumped from about 7,000 in 1914 to more than 40,000 in 1928. As Americans could afford to spend more time and money on entertainment, the number of golf courses tripled, and the number of bowling alleys increased eightfold. After satisfying their basic needs, Americans had enough left over to contribute record amounts of money to colleges and universities.

PRO-BUSINESS GOVERNMENT

A crucial factor in keeping the run of prosperity going was government policy. The man who presided over the nation for most of the twenties was considered the best friend the industrial leaders could have had.

America's booming postwar economy enabled middle-class Americans to spend more on consumer products, and on leisure activities like golf.

END OF PROSPERITY

In his last State of the Union speech on December 4, 1928, President Calvin Coolidge expressed the prevailing view of the nation's leadership that times in the United States had never been better. The passage is from Coolidge: An American Enigma, *by Robert Sobel:*

"The country is in the midst of an era of prosperity more extensive and of peace more permanent than it has ever before experienced. . . . No Congress of the United States ever assembled, in surveying the state of the union, has met with a more pleasing prospect than that which appears at the present time. In the domestic field there is tranquility and contentment, harmonious relations between management and wage earners, freedom from industrial strife, and the highest recorded years of prosperity."

Calvin Coolidge, who took over the presidency in 1923 upon the death of Warren Harding, made his priorities for the nation clear when he declared that "the business of America is business."[1] His enthusiasm for the role of industry led him to praise business as "one of the greatest contributing forces to the moral and spiritual advancement of the race."[2]

For the most part the captains of industry insisted that the best thing the government could do for the economy was follow a policy of "laissez-faire," which means to leave it alone. Charles Mitchell, president of the nation's wealthiest bank, National City Bank, expressed the sentiments of most businesspersons when he urged that business be "left to businessmen."[3]

For a pro-business president who was not inclined to use the power of the federal government unless absolutely necessary, that was easy advice to follow. The Coolidge administration was generally content to watch from the sidelines and let the marketplace dictate the course of events as big business cranked out record production and hefty profits.

On the few occasions when government stepped in, it was only to give the captains of industry an extra break. Business leaders wanted two things from their federal government: low taxes and a strong tariff. During the 1920s, the federal government cooperated on both fronts. Coolidge's manager of economic issues, Secretary of the Treasury Andrew Mellon, was himself one of the titans of the American business community, having made a fortune in oil and banking. Under his direction the government slashed taxes for corporations and the wealthiest Americans. Seldom has a conflict of interest in the federal government been more glaring, as Mellon benefited from his own policies to swell his empire from just over $1.5 billion in assets to $6 billion during his terms of office.

The tariff issue, which some American businesspeople strongly supported, took longer to resolve. A tariff is a tax on foreign goods entering the country and is used to protect domestic businesses from foreign competition. Although the issue was hotly debated, Congress did not impose the high tariff until the end of the decade.

ENTER HERBERT HOOVER

After filling out Harding's term and then serving one more term as president, Coolidge declined to run again. When he left office in 1928, U.S. voters replaced him with Herbert Hoover. Business leaders were even more optimistic about the future under Hoover than they had been under Coolidge, and they were not alone. There was no greater symbol of the United States as the land of opportunity than Hoover. He had proved the notion that any person, no matter how humble their origins, could rise

to the top if they had the ability and determination to do so.

Hoover, the son of Iowa farmers, was orphaned at age ten. He did not let the tragedy deter him from concentrating on his studies. He gained acceptance to one of the nation's top universities, Stanford, where he earned a degree in mining engineering. Entering the world of business, Hoover succeeded so quickly that he joined the ranks of the nation's millionaires before he was forty years old.

Then, Hoover began devoting his efforts to public service. His handling of the U.S. government's relief efforts in war torn Europe following World War I earned him the admiration of millions. One grateful European official publicly thanked Hoover, saying, "You have saved from death three and a half million children and five and a half million adults."[4]

When this work was completed, Hoover joined Coolidge's administration as secretary of commerce. Although it was not con-

---

TRIUMPH OVER POVERTY

In accepting the nomination of the Republican Party for president in 1928, Herbert Hoover expressed confidence that the nation was on the verge of an unprecedented achievement in world history. This passage is quoted from Herbert Hoover: A Public Life, *by David Burner:*

"We in America today are nearer to the final triumph over poverty than ever before in the history of any land. The poorhouse is vanishing from among us. . . . We shall soon with the help of God be in sight of the day when poverty shall be banished from this nation. . . . Upon the structure of material progress as a base, we are erecting a structure of idealism that would be impossible without the material base."

The economic expertise of Herbert Hoover (right), demonstrated by his outstanding performance in the cabinet of Calvin Coolidge (left), was one of many reasons Americans elected him president by a wide margin in 1928.

sidered one of the top cabinet positions, Hoover brought such energy and expertise to the job that he became one of the dominant figures in the federal government, showing a particular ability to forge effective alliances between government and business.

The American people rewarded him by electing him president by an overwhelming margin over his opponent, Democrat Al Smith. Business leaders were almost giddy with anticipation over the future under Hoover. The prominent mouthpiece of the American business community, *The Wall Street Journal*, proclaimed, "There has never been a President with a fundamental understanding of economics better than Mr. Hoover."[5]

Hoover, however, was far more than a champion of big business. Working people admired him for his humanitarian values and for his demonstrated effectiveness in relieving the suffering of the poor. The vast majority of Americans agreed with the assessment of historians Lois and Alan Gordon, who declared that Hoover was "by far the best qualified of the three presidents of the decade."[6]

The prospect of Herbert Hoover in the White House excited Americans more than virtually any inauguration of a president before his time or since. Hoover's qualifications were summed up in a September 1925 article in the New Republic, *when Hoover was serving as secretary of commerce:*

"Speaking of Hoover . . . there is reason to doubt whether in the whole history of the American government a Cabinet officer has engaged in such wide diversity of activities or covered quite so much ground.

The plain fact is that no vital problem, whether in the foreign or domestic field, arises in this administration in the handling of which Mr. Hoover does not have a real— and very often a leading— part. . . .

This is not because Hoover pushes himself forward and asks for them. A more modest, retiring man it would be hard to find—certainly here in Washington. He is doing the things he is because of the sheer knowledge and ability of the man and his extraordinary experience which has covered many fields and many parts of the world."

DECADE OF CONSUMERISM

The U.S. economic boom that Hoover inherited could not have been accomplished without a great demand for the products that industry was producing. One way to increase demand was to keep interest rates low, so consumers would be tempted to use credit to buy expensive products they could not afford to purchase outright. Another factor boosting demand was the ability of business to persuade consumers that they needed the products that industry was producing. In the 1920s, business turned to advertising for this purpose with a vengeance. For the first time in its history, more money was spent in the United States on advertising than on education.

Much of this increased spending went to a relatively recent communications medium, the radio. Prior to World War I, radios were novelties owned mainly by electronics hobbyists. On average, only ten people in a city of one hundred thousand owned one. Advances in radio technology, however, dropped the price dramatically after the war. When the news and entertainment industries latched onto the radio as a way to reach audiences, they began putting on shows that enticed millions of consumers to buy their own radios. By 1927 so many radio stations were clogging the airwaves that the Federal Radio Commission had to begin issuing licenses and assigning specific radio frequencies.

Businesses quickly learned that the radio was a fantastic tool for advertising their products. Americans found themselves bombarded as never before by persuasive arguments urging them to buy products. Inexperienced in dealing with masters of subtle sales techniques, they often accepted the arguments. Whereas previous generations of Americans were highly suspicious of buying on credit unless it was absolutely necessary, in the 1920s credit purchases and installment buying became a way of life for many middle- and even lower-class families.

The economic boom in the United States during the 1920s, then, was characterized by materialism on a mass scale, the likes of which the world had never seen. High-living, hard-partying, and extravagant shows of wealth, eagerly documented by the media, became the fashion, which led to the decade's nickname of the Roaring Twenties. In the words of author Judith S. Baughman, "The new corporate order no longer valued restraint, thrift and sobriety, but instead was oriented toward conformity, consumerism, and individual gratification."[7]

DARK SIDE OF THE ROARING TWENTIES

In many ways, however, the nickname Roaring Twenties was an exaggerated description of the decade. According to T. H. Watkins, author of several books on the era, "Most Americans most of the time did not consider themselves part of the parade of the twenties, even though an increasingly garish and inescapable mass media made it nearly impossible to ignore all the noise and circumstance."[8] In fact, even the widely advertised prosperity of the decade was, for the average American, an illusion. Despite the claims that "the business of America is business," the fact that much of the industrial community was rolling in prosperity meant nothing to the average worker.

While the wealthy industrialists raked in staggering profits, they declined to let working Americans share in the prosperity. The average hourly wage of the American worker in 1929 was sixty cents, exactly what it had been at the beginning of the decade. The bargaining position of workers was in decline, thanks in part to the dwindling influence of labor unions. Membership in trade unions had declined steeply, from around 5 million in 1920 to 3.4 million by 1929.

According to government statistics, over 90 percent of the nation's wealth in 1920 was concentrated in the pockets of 13 percent of the population. Only 5 percent of the population earned more than $6,000 a year. Incredibly, in this era widely publicized as one of prosperity, the majority of Americans were actually locked in an unending struggle for survival. The U.S. Department of Labor estimated that at the height of 1920s prosperity, between 60 and 75 percent of all American families earned less than $2,000 per year, which experts pegged as the minimum necessary to adequately support a family of four. The average factory worker took home only $1,500 a year in pay, while teachers averaged a paltry $1,277 in salary.

While big corporations amassed record profits, the small businesses that tried to compete with them failed, putting people out of work. During the course of the decade roughly twenty thousand businesses shut their doors forever each year. Even worse off than the average worker and small-business owner were the 30 million Americans who depended on farming for their livelihood, especially those in the western states. Farm income declined throughout the decade. The problem grew critical when prices for farm products plunged by 30 percent between 1925 and 1929. Coolidge's hands-off government policy offered no help to desperate farmers. By 1929 an estimated one out of every four farms had been sold to pay off debts, putting millions of farmers out of work.

The booming economy failed to create new jobs to keep up with the need for them. By the middle of 1929 national unemployment was near 5 percent and rising. In some large cities the problem was even worse. New York City, for example, had to cope with an astronomical unemployment level of 17 percent, even during the prosperous summer of 1929.

Meanwhile, the failing farms and small businesses dragged down the banking industry, particularly in rural areas. In the first twenty years of the twentieth century the number of banks going out of business averaged fewer than 90 per year. From

Although the 1920s are often remembered as a prosperous decade, farming families did not share in the economic boom. By 1929 falling prices had caused millions of farms to fail.

1923 to 1929 that average climbed to 691 per year. In 1926 alone, 976 banks shut their doors, with the farming communities of Iowa being the hardest hit.

The desperate state of many American families was worsened by the new buying habits urged on them by society and the advertising blitz. The new installment plan purchases lured many to spend more than they could afford in hopes that they would have more money in future months than at present. For most Americans, owning an automobile had come to be considered a necessity for transportation. The payments they had to shell out for a car made it even more difficult for them to live within their means.

SOCIETAL UNREST

The rosy image of prosperity in the 1920s also disguised the fact that grave potential problems were rising up in society. Prohibition had created new headaches in place of the old ones associated with alcohol consumption. Enforcement of the ban on alcohol proved futile in many areas. Federal agents (U.S. policemen, or "G-men") were easily corrupted by bribes, and demand for liquor was so high that thousands of secret alcohol-serving establishments known as speakeasies sprang up in New York City alone. Hundreds of Americans were dying from poisonous "bootleg" (homemade) alcohol they purchased on the sly to evade the rules of Prohibition. Mobsters such as Al Capone were making millions of dollars on illegal liquor sales and turning cities into violent battlegrounds between rival gangs. Al Capone and his syndicate took in an estimated $105 million in illegal profits in 1928 while terrorizing the city of Chicago.

Problems in race relations were also simmering. Following World War I, African Americans who were unable to eke out a decent living working southern farms flocked to northern cities in search of factory jobs. They were met with hostility, especially from labor unions, which hoarded the best-paying factory jobs for whites only. Resentment of minorities gave new life to the racist Ku Klux Klan organization, whose membership climbed to more than 9 million in the 1920s.

Many Americans grew concerned about the effect that the modern, materialistic, big-business-oriented society was having on the nation's character. The divorce rate rose sharply during the 1920s. Church attendance dropped. Fewer Americans showed up at the polls to vote.

Meanwhile, storm clouds of armed conflict were rising over foreign lands. The social and economic upheavals that followed World War I left much of Europe fearful, confused, and angry. Aggressive political factions took advantage of the unrest to lay claim to power. By 1929, dictators had already assumed power in Spain, Italy, Hungary, Poland, Yugoslavia, and elsewhere. A tiny radical party known as the Nazis began to attract attention in Germany.

EVERYONE OUGHT TO BE RICH

Somehow, when viewed against the background of the flourishing economy, these

*Construction mogul John Raskob
believed that the key to financial
security for average Americans was
investing in the stock market.*

problems seemed insignificant to American leaders, if they were noticed at all. In fact, many of them believed that the wave of prosperity on which the United States was riding would carry the nation, and perhaps even the world, into a new era of perpetual plenty.

"One of the oldest and perhaps the noblest of human aspirations has been the abolishment of poverty," said Herbert Hoover. "We in America today are nearer to the final triumph over poverty than ever before in the history of the land. The poor house is vanishing from among us."[9]

John Jacob Raskob, who was in the midst of planning construction of the tallest building in the world, the Empire State Building, was firmly convinced that every American could be rich within a generation. Writing in the *Ladies' Home Journal,* Raskob set out his vision of the future. "Given wide-spread prosperity," he declared, "the need for charity will diminish. A growing population largely without financial worries will raise ambitious, contented children. A great affliction is . . . want, if not actual poverty in old age. I believe that condition can be alleviated, if not abolished."

Raskob proposed what appeared to him to be a foolproof plan for eliminating poverty. "If a man saves $15 a week and invests in good common stocks, . . . at the end of 20 years, he will have at least $80,000 and $400 a month. He will be rich. And because anyone can do that, I am firm in my belief that anyone not only can be rich, but ought to be rich."[10]

Raskob made a glaring miscalculation in his proposal that demonstrated how out-of-touch he and other U.S. leaders were with the common American. Given the fact that the average worker earned only twenty-five to thirty dollars per week, the notion that they could save any money at all, let alone fifteen dollars a week, was clearly ridiculous. But Raskob's theory reflected his view that the stock market, a curious invention of financial wizards, was a miracle moneymaking machine. By the end of the 1920s, millions of Americans had reached the same conclusion.

2 Growth of the Stock Market

The idea behind the stock market was simple. Businesses needed money to finance the expansion of their facilities and workforce, and to acquire raw materials they could turn into products. The stock market provided a way to obtain these funds. The company would simply sell shares of stock to investors and use that money to build its business. In exchange, the company returned to the investors a portion of the profits it made, generally in the form of regular payments called dividends.

HISTORY OF THE NEW YORK STOCK EXCHANGE

The stock market was far from a modern idea. The New York Stock Exchange had been organized back in 1792 by a group of stockbrokers (intermediaries who arrange the sale of company stocks) looking for a more orderly and convenient way to buy and sell company stocks. Although stock exchanges also arose in other cities such as Boston and San Francisco, the New York Stock Exchange had become by far the nation's largest and most important simply by virtue of its location.

New York City had established itself as the nation's financial center in the first days of the republic. The hub of this financial activity was a short, six-block street, named Wall Street in the days when the city was a Dutch colony and a side of it had been walled off to keep out cattle from the neighboring farms. By 1802, forty banks had located their main offices on Wall Street, which was also home to the New York Stock Exchange. Eventually six of the ten largest banks in the nation would open their doors within a few blocks of the stock exchange.

This stock exchange grew slowly but steadily in size, influence, and prestige. In 1815 the selling prices of New York Stock Exchange stocks were deemed important enough to be listed regularly in the city's major newspapers. Recognizing that their exchange provided stockbrokers with a valuable way to profitably buy and sell stocks, the organizers eventually began charging for the privilege of taking part. In 1870 they began charging two thousand dollars for membership.

The New York Stock Exchange was an exclusive club. Even as late as 1929, very few firms allowed Jews to work in their companies; no blacks or women were hired except for those who did the most menial jobs.

Stock market investors experienced some rough financial bumps over the years. Occasionally the nation's business and financial climate would go sour. Businesses struggled and produced no profits, making their stocks decline in value. When that happened, investors could and did lose large sums of money. Periods of bad economic times were known as panics or depressions. The New York Stock Exchange experienced particularly bad panics in 1893 and 1907. But by and large, investors in the stock market made money, often substantial amounts.

By the twentieth century, trading in the New York Stock Exchange had become so

The New York Stock Exchange, located on Wall Street in New York City, weathered economic downturns during its rise to prominence at the turn of the twentieth century.

profitable that droves of businesses, investors, and brokers tried to get in on the action. During World War I the exchange had listed only 150 companies whose stock was for trade. By 1929 that number had swelled to over 550. There were fewer than 27,000 stockbrokers nationwide in 1920. Less than a decade later that number was conservatively estimated at 71,000. So many traders were eager to take part in the New York Stock Exchange that its directors could now charge $625,000 for membership.

THE BULL MARKET OF THE '20S

In the jargon of the stock market, a "bull" market is one in which the prices of stocks consistently go up. A "bear" market is one in which the prices consistently go down. In the 1920s the United States experienced one of the most spectacular bull markets in history. The drive for increased size led many corporations to actively pursue investors to finance their expansions. Encouraged by the enormous profitability of these growing corporations, investors eagerly snapped up the stock options that these companies offered. The greater the demand for stocks, the higher the price the stocks could command and therefore, the greater the value of the stocks.

In 1927 the Federal Reserve Board added fuel to the raging bull market on Wall Street. The Federal Reserve System was a nationwide bank control system established by the federal government in 1913 in an effort to provide stability to the economy and avoid the panics that occurred so frequently. Its main function was to provide the country with a reliable and reasonable source of credit. The Federal Reserve Board set the interest rate that the twelve Federal Reserve Banks, who controlled the nation's money supply, would charge other banks for the use of its money. This interest rate determined what each of the nine thousand state and national banks in each Federal Reserve District could afford to charge its customers.

In 1927 the Federal Reserve Board reduced its interest rates to a record low of 3.5 percent. Such a low rate encouraged massive borrowing, both by companies and investors. Along with Mellon's policy of tax cuts for corporations and the wealthy, this made it attractive for people to spend money on long-term investments such as stocks. Demand for stocks soared, as did the value of stocks, by about $75 billion from 1927 to 1929.

SPECULATION

As stock prices soared, the entire dynamic of stock market investing changed. Previously, the goal of investors had been to put money into sound companies that were likely to make a decent profit and reward the investor with dividends from that profit. But investors soon discovered that the real profits of the stock market had nothing to do with collecting dividends; the big money came from speculation.

Speculation in stocks differs from standard investment in that speculators buy stocks for the purpose of selling them within a fairly short time at a large profit. In many ways, speculation is a form of legal-

NOT TO WORRY

Unlike Hoover, President Coolidge had no concerns about the amount of loans used to finance speculation in the stock market. On January 7, 1928, he gave this analysis of the situation, quoted in Coolidge: An American Enigma *by Robert Sobel, which illustrates both his optimism and his reluctance to interfere with the affairs of business:*

"I am not familiar enough with the exact workings and practice of the Federal Reserve System so that comments that I might make relating to the amount of broker's loans would not be of very much value. I do know in a general way that the amount of securities in the country has increased very largely in recent years. The number of different securities that are dealt in on the stock exchange are very much larger than they were previously. The deposits in the banks also are larger. And those two things together would necessarily be a reason for doing more business of a kind that is transacted by brokers and would naturally result in a larger sum of money being used for that purpose. Now, whether the amount at the present time is disproportionate to the resources of the country, I am in no position to judge accurately, but so far as indicated by an inquiry that I have made of the Treasury Department and so on, I haven't had any indication that the amount was large enough to cause particularly unfavorable comment."

---

ized gambling: the investor is basically betting that a stock they purchased today can be sold for much more money in a few years or even months.

Throughout much of the 1920s, those who speculated in the stock market were richly rewarded. Prices rose steadily higher, sometimes spectacularly higher. In July 1929, for example, values of stocks on the New York Stock Exchange rose an average of nearly 7 percent. On an annual basis, that figures out to an 85 percent return on investment, as opposed to the 3 to 5 percent return that people could make from other investments such as dividends, bonds, or bank accounts. Selected individual stocks bestowed even more astonishing profits. During the summer of 1929, Westinghouse jumped from $151 a share to $286. General Electric leapt from $268 a share to $391. American Telephone & Telegraph (AT&T) rose from $209 a share to $303, and at one point its stock gained a total of $75 million in value in a single day!

TRICKS OF THE TRADE

Those with business savvy found ingenious ways to take advantage of the bull market to

GOING FOR THE FAST BUCK

Highly regarded economist John Maynard Keynes worked out some of his famous financial theories during the stock market boom of the 1920s. Here is his brief analysis of the effects of speculation on the business climate, quoted in The Day the Bubble Burst, *by Gordon Thomas and Max Morgan-Witts:*

"Amid the rapid fluctuations of his fortunes, the businessman loses his conservative instincts, and begins to think more of the large gains of the moment than of the lesser, but permanent, profits of normal business. The welfare of his enterprise in the relatively distant future weighs less with him than before, and thoughts are excited of a quick fortune and clearing out."

amass even more staggering fortunes. One of the most effective methods, of which Will Durant was a master, was the investment pool. The investment pool was a collaborative effort of a group of wealthy investors. Rather than purchasing stocks individually, these investors, which included bankers and other corporate leaders, joined together to buy huge chunks of stocks in selected companies. By placing these enormous purchase orders, the investment pools instantly created a large demand for these stocks. Since the price of stocks rises and falls according to the demand, the effect of their bulk purchases was to increase the price of the stock. Often, an unsuspecting public would see a sudden rise in the value of a stock and conclude that this was an enormously popular and profitable stock, worth owning. Many of them would then try to purchase these same stocks. The more people interested in purchasing the stock, the more the value of the stock would rise.

Within a short period of time the stock would be worth considerably more than what the investment pool participants had paid for it. Knowing that they had created an artificial demand that inflated the price of the stock far above its true value, the investment pool quickly sold their stocks before the price could drop. Many times they pocketed outlandish profits from their brief ownership of the stock. For example, in 1928 an investment pool started buying large blocks of Radio Company of America (RCA) stock. They created such a demand for the stock that its price rose from $79 a share to $109 a share in just ten days. The investment pool immediately sold its stock and divided millions of dollars of almost instant profit among the pool members.

The questionable ethics of pumping up a stock price to fool the public into joining the bandwagon did not bother the consciences of the investment pool operators. As banking giant J. P. Morgan said when such tactics were questioned, "God wouldn't have made sheep if he didn't expect them to be sheared."[11]

Another business strategy was the organization of holding companies. A holding company is a corporation that does not manufacture any product; it exists only to control stock in other companies. Many companies formed separate holding companies to take advantage of tax laws relating to the stock market. By 1929, about one out of every five corporations trading on the New York Stock Exchange was a holding company. Holding companies dominated certain sectors of the business community. Nine powerful holding companies, for example, controlled the stock of three-fourths of the nation's power resources.

A third complex investment strategy was the practice of buying on margin. This was a purely speculative activity that depended heavily on stock market prices rising. A person buying on margin would not buy the stock outright. Instead, he or she would put up a portion of the money and borrow the rest, usually from a stockbroker.

Investment pool operators purchased large blocks of stock in companies like RCA in order to increase demand for the stock, and then sold their shares for a quick and substantial profit.

As an example, a person would pay $1,000 for stocks valued at $4,000, and borrow the remaining amount from the broker. If the stocks' value increased to $8,000, the investor could then sell the stocks, pay off the $3,000 he owed to the broker, plus interest, and walk off with $4,000 in profit.

Many times investors used the profit from one margin account to invest in another. In this example, the investor would take the $4,000 profit from the first deal and put it back in the stock market. His $4,000 would allow him to purchase $16,000 worth of stock on margin, with the broker loan covering the remaining $12,000. If this

Investors in the 1920s often borrowed money to finance their stock purchases.

stock doubled in value to $32,000, he could sell the stock and pay off the $12,000 broker loan. This would leave him with a $20,000 profit from an original investment of only $1,000. In other words, margin buying allowed a person to reap a tremendous profit from only a very small investment.

The danger in margin buying was that the investor could be in serious trouble if the stock market went down. If the investor put up $1,000 for stock valued at $4,000, the broker's loan of the remaining $3,000 would begin to look very risky if the stock price dropped. If the stock value slipped to $3,000, the amount of the broker's loan equaled the entire value of the stock. That would put the broker at risk of losing money if the price went down further. In order to prevent this, the broker would require the investor to invest more of his money to reduce the amount of the loan. This was known as a margin call.

In the above case, if the investor could not come up with the extra money to cover the margin call, the broker would have to sell the stock at its current price. If the price had fallen to $2,000, he would lose $1,000 of his $3,000 loan, while the investor lost his entire $1,000 investment. As the price of stocks climbed steadily in the late 1920s, however, most investors believed that the potential gains of margin investing were easily worth the risk.

WALL STREET INVESTORS AS CELEBRITIES

By the summer of 1929 the profits that investors were gaining with their ingenious strategies were so astounding that even the most conservative businesspeople found it hard to resist following their lead. In the words of Tom Shachtman, "the New York Stock Exchange had become the focus of business experts and a means of expanding income that was unparalleled in intensity throughout the world."[12]

Under the circumstances, the time-honored virtue of saving money in a bank seemed to many to be hopelessly out of date. Control of the financial world passed from the bankers to the aggressive and brash financial wizards.

As stock profits soared, the activities of the New York Stock Exchange began to take over the front pages of the newspapers. Day after day, newspaper and magazine columns highlighted stories of business tycoons who made a killing in the stock market. George F. Baker of the First National Bank of New York, for example, was said to have made a profit of $11 million in just five hours.

Suddenly, Americans began looking differently at the formerly faceless men in suits who operated in the bewildering world of high finance. The stock market and the men who made fortunes investing in it became one of the main topics of conversation on street corners, parlors, and barbershops. The average person viewed the financial high rollers not with bitterness or disdain, but with envy. As Shachtman noted, "The heroes of the age were the businessmen, men who made and worked in the affluent society. Those men, almost universally, had been turning to the stock market the last several years. A European observer noted that although European stock markets reflected the economies of their countries in a steady, conservative fashion, the American stock markets had a different function—they led the economy of the country."[13] A major women's magazine even reported that its readers considered stockbrokers a match for movie stars as far as sex appeal.

GET RICH QUICK PHILOSOPHY

It was not only the wealthy giants of the investment world who made fortunes on the New York Stock Exchange. The newspapers were full of stories of ordinary working people who struck a gold mine by putting their savings in the stock market. A stenographer bought General Motors stock just when it began to skyrocket. After holding the stock for only two days she sold it for a $15,000 profit. A waiter at the New York Stock Exchange Luncheon Club earned $90,000 in the market from tips passed on to him by his customers. Everyone knew stories of widows, poor working men and women, and small-shop owners who made more money in a few years in the stock market than they had earned in their entire lives. Some of the glowing press coverage of the stock market was blatantly self-serving. Some supposedly unbiased financial reporters received secret payments for promoting certain stocks in their stories.

Nevertheless, such stories took their toll on the American work ethic. Average wage-earners in the United States could work hard all their lives and never get anywhere financially. Despite the promise of the American Dream, few Americans were able to work themselves into a comfortable position. With wages below the poverty line, a man could put in thirty or forty years of backbreaking effort and barely be able to put food on the table and a roof over his family's head, much less put aside funds for a comfortable retirement.

In such an environment, these people heard of others just like themselves who were able to break out of this dreary existence. They saw that fortunes were not being made by thrifty people who went without any luxuries in life and carefully set aside money in a savings account. Riches were not coming to people by virtue of their hard work, dependability, and dedication. Rather they came by good fortune in a sudden shower of blessings. Many began to view the stock market as the one way that ordinary people could hope to advance their financial situation. Nor were they content with making modest returns on their investments. The stories of the fortunes made on Wall Street spurred many people to throw caution to the wind in hopes of hitting a big jackpot.

ENTER THE MIDDLE-CLASS INVESTOR

Prior to World War I, few middle-class Americans had dabbled in the mysterious art of investing other than opening a savings account. They not only avoided any dealings with the Wall Street crowd but were highly suspicious and scornful of them. As far as they were concerned the stock market was just a shell game thought up by millionaires to bilk gullible customers out of their hard-earned money.

But during the war the U.S. government, in need of funds to finance the enormous cost of the military, put on a broad campaign to attract investment money from ordinary Americans. It sold what it called Liberty Bonds, which it advertised as both a patriotic duty and a win-win situation for everyone. The government needed the money in its time of emergency, so Americans had a duty to come to the aid of their country. In return for the use of their money, the government promised to repay the money with interest once the war was over.

The millions of average Americans who purchased Liberty Bonds discovered that

During World War I, middle-class Americans invested in U.S. Liberty Bonds.

WALL STREET OPTIMISM

The Wall Street Journal *has long been considered the nation's authoritative newspaper on financial concerns. On September 3, 1929, an editorial in the paper gave its assessment of the condition of the stock market, quoted in* The Day the Bubble Burst, *by Gordon Thomas and Max Morgan-Witts:*

"Wall Street entered the autumn financial season in a definitely optimistic frame of mind. With railroad traffic showing steady gains, and production in the major branches of industry continuing at a high rate, the earnings prospects of the principal corporations with shares listed on the Stock Exchange were looked upon as extremely promising. Sentiment regarding the credit outlook was reassured by the activities of the Federal Reserve authorities in placing funds at the disposal of business through bill purchases in the open market. With trade and credit conditions favorable, buying orders accumulated in large volume over Labor Day, and the forward movement in the main body of stocks was vigorously resumed in the early dealings. . . . While irregularity cropped out from time to time during the day, due to profit-taking attracted by the sweeping character of the recent gains, the main upward trend was fairly well sustained throughout the session."

financial investing was not as complicated and risky as they had thought. In fact, it could be profitable. Having lost their fear of investing, and spurred by reports of the wealth to be achieved in the stock market, they were willing to try their hand at this activity.

The stock market was just as eager to welcome them. The tremendous expansion needs of U.S. industry meant that companies were looking to attract huge infusions of funds, which they solicited with new issues of stock. Advertising campaigns, making use of the new radio audience, urged

the public to take advantage of this fool-proof moneymaking opportunity.

The public snapped up new stock offerings as fast as they appeared. The total number of shares traded on the New York Stock Exchange jumped from 173 million in 1921 to 920 million in 1928. In fact, according to financier Jesse Livermore, stock market investing turned into "a new national sport which can be played for the price of an evening paper."[14] By the end of the 1920s, stockbrokers were opening offices in communities throughout the nation. Even working-class people invested what little savings they had in the stock market, often buying on margin to increase their purchasing power.

The number of small investors grew daily. During 1929 there was a 65 percent increase in the number of people owning stocks, with most of the increase coming from the ranks of lower income workers. The largest increase in stockholders was among women. Before the mid-1920s, few women had anything to do with the stock market. By 1929 there were five thousand stockbrokers in the United States who specialized in women clients. Women owned more than half the total stock of some of the nation's largest corporations, such as AT&T and the Pennsylvania Railroad.

INVESTMENT TRUSTS

For the first time in its history, the New York Stock Exchange was catering to investors who had little idea of how the stock market worked. Many of these novices tended to trust the market judgment and savvy of the large investors. They would follow the market trends established by wealthy investors and invest in whatever seemed to be the most popular with the experts. But for investors who had neither knowledge of the market nor the time to analyze its ups and downs, stockbrokers offered the investment trust.

The investment trust was an idea that came to the United States from Great Britain in 1920. It was basically a business service set up to manage funds for unsophisticated small investors. Like an investment pool, it combined the resources of many investors, except that the investors purchased shares in the investment trust rather than in individual stocks. The investment trust then invested these funds in stocks selected by its operators. With professionals in charge of their money, small investors did not have to worry about

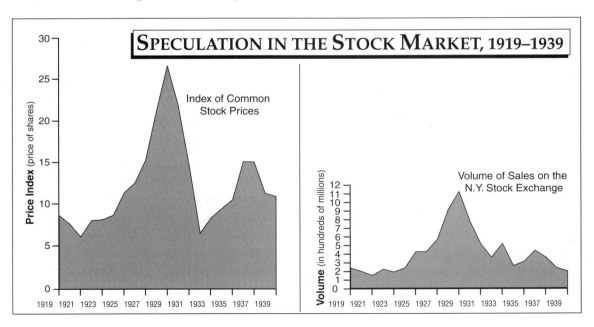

SPECULATION IN THE STOCK MARKET, 1919–1939

Index of Common Stock Prices

Volume of Sales on the N.Y. Stock Exchange

learning the trends and operating procedures of the market. Furthermore, the investment trusts offered protection to investors in the form of diversification. With the large amount of funds at their disposal, trust managers could invest in a wide range of stocks. Rather than depending on one stock or a few stocks to do well, the investment trust spread the risk over many companies. That way, if a company went bad, as could happen even in times when most stocks were soaring in price, investors would not lose their entire investment. The loss would be more than canceled out by gains made by other, profitable, stocks in the investment trust portfolio.

The professionalism of these trusts varied widely. Some were managed by sharp operators who had little business knowledge or experience. Nevertheless, by the end of the decade, Americans were stampeding into the perceived shelter of investment trusts. In 1927 a total of 160 such trusts were working in the stock market. The following year 140 more came into existence, and 265 started up in 1929. By that time an estimated 4 to 5 million Americans had placed money in these trusts. With such an enormous demand for stocks, their prices continued to climb, handsomely rewarding many investors.

3 Danger Signs

As the bull market roared into 1929, most people expected the good times to continue. Early in the year, outgoing president Coolidge declared that even though stock prices had risen dramatically, they were still cheap at current prices. The arrival of Herbert Hoover in office only swelled the optimism. The prevailing view was that if the economy thrived under a very ordinary president like Coolidge, imagine what would happen during the watch of an administrative wizard like Hoover.

During the summer the *Wall Street Journal*, considered the authority on financial news, noted, "The outlook for the fall months seems brighter than at any time in recent years."[15] Yale University's highly respected economics professor, Irving Fisher, seconded that analysis, saying that he expected "to see the stock market a good deal higher than it is today within a few months."[16]

For those with a more mystical view of the world, the words of Evangeline Adams, the most noted astrologer of the time, provided even more encouragement. In the summer of 1929 she predicted that "the Dow Jones could climb to heaven."[17] (The Dow Jones average is the average advance or decline in the prices of a sample group of influential stocks. Economic analysts use it as a quick method of measuring stock market activity.) All of these positive statements encouraged investors to trust that the stock market would continue to rise.

Economist Irving Fisher, like most experts, predicted that stock prices would continue to rise throughout 1929.

Respected international banker Paul Warburg was one of the few arguing that the government, via the Federal Reserve System, needed to take action to curtail speculation on Wall Street. He spoke these words, quoted in 1929: The Year of the Great Crash, *by William Klingaman, in March 1929:*

"When the savings of the masses are deposited as margins for Stock Exchange speculations, and when the extravagant use of funds for speculative purposes absorbs so much of the nation's credit supply that it threatens to cripple the country's regular business, then there does not seem to be any doubt as to the direction in which the Federal Reserve System ought to exercise its influence quickly and forcefully. . . . If orgies of unrestrained speculation are permitted to spread too far, however, the ultimate collapse is certain not only to affect the speculators themselves, but also to bring about a general depression involving the entire country."

Furthermore, small investors and brokers believed they were playing it safe by swimming along with the major financial powers. In their view, the big banks and wealthy investors had too much at stake in the bull market to allow it to end. The instant demand started to wane, these business giants would pour more of their own wealth into the market to create new demand and stabilize prices.

PERILS OF SPECULATION

Yet there were certain aspects of the nation's mania for the stock market that made some experts uneasy. Chief among these concerns was the fact that speculation was a dangerous game. Although stocks were enjoying unprecedented success, the basic rules of economics had not changed: for every buyer there has to be a seller, and for every seller a buyer. Stocks could command high prices and could continue to rise in value only because, at this time, people were eager to buy them. But what would happen if demand fell? What if people could not find anyone interested in buying stock for which they had paid thousands of dollars?

Over the centuries that scenario had come to pass many times and in many forms. One of the most famous of these speculation busts occurred in Holland in the 1700s, when the nation was swept by a craze for certain varieties of tulips. Demand was so high that prices for these plants skyrocketed and speculators made a fortune—for a while. Eventually, though, the price for tulips rose higher than people could afford. Demand dropped off, prices plunged, and suddenly thousands of speculators found themselves ruined. The same pattern had occurred frequently in the United States in real estate. Many Americans had been badly burned speculating in wilderness real estate because they believed that land-hungry settlers would pay premium prices for such land. They found themselves stuck with the property and saddled with huge debts when no one turned up to buy.

Experts noted that the potential for disaster in stock market speculation was especially high because the market was saturated with small investors who had unrealistic expectations of winning a fortune and had not the slightest idea of how the stock market worked. If things started to go bad, they could not be expected to understand what was happening or know what to do to minimize their losses. There was a good chance they would panic, and nothing is more dangerous to a stock market than panic among the investors. In a panic, prices can go into a free fall.

Furthermore, millions of these naive investors were speculating by buying stocks on margin. In other words, many of them were buying a great deal of stock they did not have the cash to pay for. As long as stock values were rising, this caused no problem. But a falling market could trigger a chain reaction of panic that would devastate the market. As Judith Baughman describes the risk: "In the worst case, if the stock kept falling, the customer ultimately ran out of cash, and the broker, who in most cases had himself borrowed money from his banker, was forced to sell the account for what he could get. The greater the margin, the greater the difficulty when the market began to fall. If the customer could not pay the brokers, the broker was unable to pay the banker, and all parties fell like a house of cards."[18]

HIDDEN DESTRUCTIVE EFFECTS OF SPECULATION

Many of the worst problems associated with stock speculation were far more subtle than the possibility of a stock market panic. One of the most insidious problems was that speculation took money away from productive enterprises. Many small businesspersons and farmers needed loans to tide them over difficult times or to help them expand to make their businesses competitive. Bankers and other investors, however, saw that they could make a far greater return on their money by either putting it into the stock market or loaning it as call money to stock market investors who were willing to pay exorbitant rates in order to get in on the Wall Street action. Even banks that were inclined to serve their local communities had fewer deposits they could loan out because so many of their customers were emptying their savings accounts to invest in the stock market.

That left farmers and small businesspersons, particularly in the Midwest, without any way to finance their operations. Meanwhile, big businesses were awash in cash from the sale of their stock offerings and they used it to undertake massive expansion and modernization. This gave big firms a huge advantage over small enterprises and helped drive the small operators out of business in record numbers.

With farmers and small businesspersons floundering, production in much of the nation slowed to a crawl.

Another complex problem with speculation concerned overseas markets. World War I had devastated the economies of much of Europe. In the early 1920s, U.S. banks and investors loaned billions of dollars to these nations to help them rebuild their industries. But as speculation fever hit Wall Street in 1927, most investors began to pull their loans out of Europe and transfer their investments to the stock market, where the rate of return was far higher.

Not only did this hurt the European nations by derailing their economic recovery, but it eventually came back to bite the U.S. economy. In the 1920s the United States' major industries expanded so quickly that they began to produce more than the American public could buy. One remedy for this problem would have been for U.S. companies to develop new markets for their products in Europe. But by pulling

European countries' economies were shattered by post World War I inflation. A German newspaper vendor collects her money in a laundry basket.

their loans out of Europe, U.S. investors slowed the European recovery and made it difficult for Europeans to afford American products. U.S. industry was left with few markets to buy their surplus production.

GOVERNMENT CONCERN OVER SPECULATION

In 1929 some federal government officials including President Hoover were keenly concerned over the dangers of rampant stock market speculation. Hoover had been quietly warning since 1926 that unrestrained speculation could lead to an economic depression. Members of the Federal Reserve Board had become increasingly nervous about the issue. Treasury Secretary Mellon had joined the ranks of those who viewed speculation as a danger.

The problem was what to do about it. This was an era in which the prevailing opinion was that government should stay out of the realm of business as much as possible. In 1928 the Federal Reserve Board made a halfhearted effort to discourage speculative loans by slightly raising the interest rate it charged member banks. On February 1, 1929, the Federal Reserve tried a different approach by issuing an advisory against further speculation in the stock market. These mild remedies had little effect on the epidemic of speculations other than to scare away a few investors and trigger a brief dip in stock market prices. But they drew the wrath of the business community. The *Wall Street Journal* went so far as to say that, even though the Federal Reserve was created specifically to protect the public against financial panics, it had no business trying to regulate activity in the stock market.

In such a hands-off climate, officials such as Mellon were reluctant to even hint that there was any cause for concern over specu-

---

SHOCK EFFECTS

In the June 1929 issue of Atlantic Monthly, *government spokesman Howard Douglas Dozier outlined the danger of speculative buying that relied so heavily on a continuing upward stock market trend:*

"Just what would be the result if that state of the public mind which has made possible the present inflation of stock prices should receive a sudden shock? . . . Should some mishap befall the stock market, each (private corporation which had leant call money) would be so busy saving himself that he would have scant time or inclination to save others. . . . The calling of the loans made to brokers by a half-dozen or so large corporations, if the calls should be made simultaneously, would shock the stock market."

Treasury Secretary Andrew Mellon was concerned about widespread speculation in the stock market.

lation in the stock market. Mellon feared that any such public pronouncement would discourage people from investing and thereby end the bull market.

Hoover's policy was to try to bring about the needed changes in the financial world by private persuasion, not by government action. When he became president, he publicly encouraged people to consider forms of investment other than stocks and asked banks to exercise care in loaning money for speculation. He encouraged financial journalists to use the power of the press to caution the public against speculation. These voluntary measures, however, had no apparent effect.

In March the Federal Reserve Board went a small step further by sending letters to its reserve banks asking them to refuse further loans for all speculation. Again, this mildest of remedies sent a tremor through the stock market. The mere idea that the Federal Reserve was suggesting that restrictions might be placed on money loaned out for margin speculation put those who needed loans to play the market in a bind. There was still a huge demand for speculation money, and with the sources of those loans in danger of drying up, competition for those funds grew fierce. Lenders could charge almost whatever they wanted, and at one point the loan rate for stock market margin buying jumped to 20 percent interest.

On March 25 trading was furious at the New York Stock Exchange as inexperienced investors were scared into unloading their stocks. The value of many stocks plunged twenty to thirty points before the day was over. As the value of stocks fell, those who had bought them on margin ran into trouble. Lenders issued calls for them to put up more money to secure the loans. Some of those who did not have the cash to cover those margin calls lost their entire investment.

Fearing that meddling by the Federal Reserve was ruining the bull market that was making them wealthy, many lenders resisted the Federal Reserve's request. Foremost among these was Charles Mitchell, chairman of the board of National City Bank, the largest bank in the nation. Mitchell did just the opposite of what the Federal Reserve requested; his bank immediately made available $25 million in call money. This announcement soothed the nerves of jittery investors. Even though some banks reduced the amount of the speculative loans, corporations and wealthy individuals stepped in to meet the

National City Bank chairman Charles Mitchell defied a Federal Reserve Board request that banks stop issuing loans for margin speculation.

demand. By the end of the trading day, the interest rate on call money had dropped to 15 percent, and the stock market staged a late rally. Reluctant to enforce its directives, the Federal Reserve could only sit and watch as the financial community hailed Mitchell as a hero for saving the stock market from what they considered to be the inept bungling of the Federal Reserve.

ROLLER-COASTER MARKET

The brief scare of late March was the first of many wild swings that rocked the stock market throughout the rest of 1929. Several times the average price of stocks dove as investors grew nervous about the speculation warnings and the government's efforts to curb the practice. In May, reports that the Federal Reserve was considering raising interest rates brought on a harrowing plunge in the market. Stocks on the New York exchange lost a combined $3 billion in a couple of days.

On August 8, the Federal Reserve Board stunned Wall Street experts who had hoped it had learned its lesson about meddling in the market. Jittery over news that the amount of brokers' loans to stock market investors had now climbed to over $6 billion, the Federal Reserve felt it had no choice but to try to discourage loans by raising its interest rate from 5 to 6 percent. Again, panic selling produced a dip in the market that wiped out a number of small speculators.

Each time the stock market plunged, however, optimism about the stock market and the strength of U.S. businesses caused it to rebound to even greater heights. Demand for stocks and the loans to buy them soared ever higher. In the summer of 1929, normally a quiet period for the New York exchange, buy orders flooded broker offices.

The roller-coaster market increased the complacency of many investors. The economy seemed so strong that the stock market was able to withstand these temporary setbacks. In fact, it appeared to act something like a balloon in the water. The further it got pushed down, the higher it shot up when it recovered. The falling of prices was not a matter for concern but simply an opportunity to get in quickly and buy stocks at bargain rates before the price rebounded.

Those familiar with European markets, however, found something disturbing about this roller-coaster market. Europe had experienced its own bull market run in past years. A similar period of wild fluctuation in market prices had occurred just before the European market dropped into a bear market.

BULL MARKET—ILLUSION?

During much of 1929, the press and the public were captivated by spectacular stories of successful stocks. Between late March and September, U.S. Steel climbed from $138 a share to $279. RCA raced from $85 to $420. These high-profile stocks produced enormous profits for their stockholders. Investors in these stocks saw their value multiply two, three, four, and even fivefold within the year. The galloping glamor stocks boosted stock indices such as the Dow Jones average to record highs by September.

Closer analysis, however, showed that the averages presented a misleading picture of the stock market's health. Heavily weighted by the influence of the giant, successful corporations, the averages gave the impression that anyone who invested in the stock market stood to make fantastic gains. In fact, during the supposedly prosperous market advance of 1929, most stocks actually lost value. In May, a study of 1,002 stocks on the New York Stock Exchange found that 614 were selling for less than they had a year earlier. When the stock market hit the peak of its success on September 3, only 388 of the nearly 1,200 issues trading in New York were selling for more than they did in January. More than 600 had lost value and were continuing to slip. In other words, during one of the most famous bull markets of all time, most stocks trading on the exchange were losing money for their investors. Since these losses were masked in the averages by the success of a few giant stocks, many unsophisticated investors had no idea that they stood a good chance of losing money if they chose the wrong stocks.

ECONOMIC SLIPPAGE

During 1929, disturbing reports trickled in hinting that the nation's economy was not as healthy as the investment community claimed. During March the nation's building construction, railroad shipping, and coal production all showed a decline. Agricultural production went into a tailspin, followed that summer by a slump in the textile industry.

By fall, most heavy industries, including the massive automobile industry, reported high inventories, meaning that they were making products faster than they could find buyers for them. In early September even one of the giants of U.S. industry, U.S. Steel, announced that it would have to cut back production. The National Association of Manufacturers reported that 40 percent of all factories in the country were now producing at a loss—they had manufactured so many products that they could not get rid of them even if they offered to sell them below cost. At the end of September the federal government discovered that the nation's exports had fallen, and business failures were on the rise. In October two key indicators of economic health, freight car loadings and housing starts, showed a marked decline.

By the fall of 1929 U.S. automakers were manufacturing more cars than they could sell.

PESSIMISTS AND PROPHETS OF DOOM

Some experts recognized that these signs pointed toward trouble. Chief among the pessimists was Massachusetts economist Roger Babson. As early as 1926, Babson had predicted that a stock market crash was coming soon and that it would have catastrophic consequences for the nation's economy. The problem with Babson and his supporters was that they had cried wolf too many times. While Babson kept predicting impending disaster in 1927 and 1928, the stock market continued to climb ever higher. Before long, most professional stock market investors dismissed him as a quirky prophet of gloom and doom.

The one time Babson made a major impact on the market was on September 5, 1929. Looking for a fresh angle on a slow news day, New York reporters played up a speech by Babson in which he repeated his belief that "sooner or later a crash is com-

ing, and it might be terrific."[19] The stark contrast between this economist's words and the soaring stock market piqued the interest of newspaper editors, who placed Babson's comments on front pages that morning.

Unsophisticated investors who had not heard of Babson's long-standing views on the subject reacted fearfully to the press hype. Frantic orders to sell bombarded the stock market floor. The sudden drop in demand for stocks sent prices reeling. Hastily, financial leaders brought in Yale's Irving Fisher to dispute everything Babson had said. Whether it was Fisher's comments or simply investors recovering their composure after the brief frenzy, the New York Stock Exchange regained most of its losses in a two-week rally.

The public's relentless demand for stocks despite rising interest rates and unfavorable economic news made a number of savvy, wealthy investors take a second look at the stock market. Leery of the growing number

Some wealthy investors, like Bernard Baruch, reacted to growing volatility in the stock market by selling their stock holdings.

of large, unpredictable swings in stock market prices, multimillionaire investor Bernard Baruch began selling most of his stock in September 1929. "A nation's economy cannot be healthy when a basic element is sick,"[20] he told his friends and associates. On his advice, many of them, such as humorist Will Rogers, pulled their money out of the market.

According to legend, Joseph Kennedy, the well-to-do father of future president John Kennedy, decided to get out of the market when a shoeshine boy offered advice on buying certain stock. Kennedy figured that if ordinary people claimed to know more about the workings of the market than he, it was time to look for a different way to make money. Other sources say that the story was an embellishment and that Kennedy acted on the advice of an adviser. Either way, in 1929, Kennedy quietly began unloading all of his stock.

Other voices of caution included A. P. Giannini. The founder of a San Francisco banking empire and a man with a passion for public service, Giannini pleaded with small-time investors to avoid risking their money on stocks. Kuhn, Loeb and Company, the second largest investment banking company on Wall Street, decided in late 1929 to get out of the stock speculation market. Even though they could charge the going rate of 14 percent for stock margin loans, the firm concluded that it would be safer to put their money in bonds paying around 5 percent.

IGNORING THE WARNINGS

Some politicians also reacted to what they saw as economic storm clouds. Herbert Hoover privately cautioned those around him to prepare for an economic slump. Senator William King of Utah proposed that Congress should step in and outlaw stock trading on margin. Virginia senator Carter Glass designed a proposal that would dampen speculation without outlawing it. He suggested that Congress slap a 5 percent tax on all transfers of stock certificates held for fewer than sixty days.

Despite warnings from financial experts and attempts by government to discourage speculation, the demand for stocks continued to be strong in September 1929 as the public buys stock at a curb exchange in New York City.

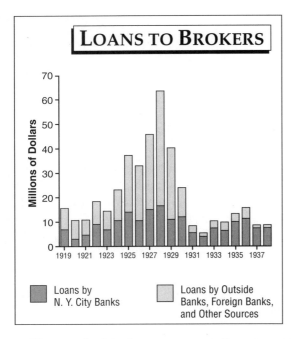

LOANS TO BROKERS

Millions of Dollars

70
60
50
40
30
20
10
0

1919 1921 1923 1925 1927 1929 1931 1933 1935 1937

■ Loans by N. Y. City Banks

☐ Loans by Outside Banks, Foreign Banks, and Other Sources

The pessimists, however, were the exceptions. Most of the financial community reacted with fury to Glass and King, and their proposals for government intervention in private business never had a chance. Armed with statistics of the stock market's continual rise, business leaders and brokers assured the public that nothing had changed and that stocks were still an outstanding investment. They reminded people that prophets of doom such as Babson had been predicting disaster for years while the stock market hummed along at a record pace. On September 20, Charles Mitchell proclaimed that "things have never been better."[21]

By and large the public agreed with him and ignored the pessimists. In September, companies continued to respond to the demand for stocks by issuing nearly $1 million more in new stocks than had been issued in any previous September. The amount of money loaned by brokers to stock investors rose past $6 billion.

Chapter

4 The Foundation Begins to Crumble

The end of September saw a continuation of drastic price swings in the New York Stock Exchange. Average prices of stocks nose-dived on September 25, followed by another vigorous rally as investors took advantage of the dip in prices to buy stocks at bargain prices. There was one difference, however, between the latest seesawing and the fluctuations that had taken place all year. Although the change went virtually unnoticed by the public, the market was not rebounding with its usual vigor. Even the latest rally failed to bring the market back up to the peak prices it had reached on September 3.

PRESSURES MOUNT AGAINST STOCK INVESTING

In late September the Bank of England caused further concern on Wall Street when it announced that it was raising the interest rates it would pay to investors. This action was matched by banks in several other European nations including Austria, Norway,

---

SITUATION SOUND

On August 21, Bernard Baruch, who was in Scotland at the time, received this cable from financier Charles Mitchell, quoted in Bernard Baruch: The Adventures of a Wall Street Legend, *by James Grant, in which Mitchell showed blissful ignorance of the impending disaster that was about to befall the stock market:*

"General situation looks exceptionally sound. Believe credit situation practically unaffected by discount rate action. Money seasonably weak. Should strengthen as the month closes. Strength in stock market centers largely on specialties, which in many cases seem unduly high, while there are many stocks, such as copper and motors and certain rails that look unjustifiably low. I doubt if anything that will not affect business can affect the market, which is like a weather-vane pointing into a gale of prosperity."

Sweden, Denmark, and Ireland. These countries took that step to counteract the harmful effect of the U.S. stock market on their economies. With many U.S. stocks offering such an attractive rate of return (profit), foreign investors had pulled their money out of their native countries and poured it into the New York Stock Exchange. As a result, these countries were now cash-poor and having difficulty financing their own industries. By raising interest rates, these foreign banks hoped to lure back investment.

This meant that several forces were now working together to discourage the demand for stocks in U.S. companies. European banks were actively competing against the New York Stock exchange for investors. The U.S. Federal Reserve had made it more difficult for people to borrow money to purchase stocks by raising its interest rates from a low of 3.5 percent in 1928 to 6 percent. The high cost of loans made speculation more risky and had put the millions of investors who purchased stocks on margin in a precarious position should the value of stocks fall. Finally, major sectors of the U.S. economy were stalling out due to overproduction and lack of markets. This was certain to affect industry profits and reduce the value of stocks. A committee of the Investment Bankers Association in New York felt compelled to issue a warning to its customers that speculation in public service stocks "has reached the danger point and many stocks are selling far above their intrinsic value."[22]

THE SLIDE

On October 3 and 4, the New York Stock Exchange suffered another significant price drop. Again, it rallied over the following week, but still did not approach the previous peaks of early September. Meanwhile, each market plunge forced brokers to ask investors to ante up more money to support their margin loans. Those investors who had risked most of their savings in the stock market and had no money to meet these margin calls had to sell out. The bouncing stock market was gradually winnowing out small investors.

THE SOUND OF FEAR

Economic reporter Matthew Josephson gave this firsthand report of the panic that hit Wall Street with such fury on October 24, quoted in The Hungry Years, *by T. H. Watkins:*

"I heard—and can still hear it—the sound of running feet, the sound of fear, as people hastened to reach posts of observation before the gong rang for the opening of trading. Hypnotized by their panic, the crowds in the boardrooms stared in horror at the stockboards or the tape recording their progressive ruin."

The buying public, however, seemed unconcerned with the stock market fluctuations. Many months of galloping stock prices and the claims of the business community that the economy was thriving as never before immunized them against concern. Even with the market's uncertain performance and the fact that most investors had actually been losing money since early September, they continued to seek out loans so they could play the market. By mid-October the total amount of broker loans had swelled to more than $7.8 billion and was still growing at the rate of $88 million a week.

Meanwhile, the stock market continued its slide. The week of October 15 ended disastrously as, in only a half day of trading on Saturday the nineteenth, the average share in the New York Stock Exchange lost all the gains made that week.

When the stock exchange reopened on Monday, the twenty-first, there was more bad news. The foreign banks' strategy of raising interest rates appeared to be having an effect. Some foreign investors had begun pulling out of the U.S. stock markets. Stock prices slid further during morning trading. In the afternoon the market rallied as it had always done in recent years after any drop in prices, and prices continued to climb Tuesday morning. This time, however, the rally stalled just as it was getting established. By Tuesday afternoon stock prices had lost every bit of the gains made in the short-lived rally.

WEDNESDAY THE TWENTY-THIRD

Even at this point, few stock market analysts saw any cause for alarm. Many of the nation's wealthiest and shrewdest businesspersons had fortunes tied up in the stock market; the consensus was that they would pour more money into the market if demand got too low. One had to expect ups and downs in the stock market, the experts noted. They continued to expect prices to rebound and resume their upward trend of the past several years. Brokerage houses continued to view the market's decline as a normal fluctuation and insisted that it was a good time to pick up bargain stocks that had slid lower than their true value. Most investors fully expected Wednesday, October 23, to be a good day for the stock market.

Instead they were stunned by a barrage of orders to sell. A record 6.3 million shares changed hands at the New York Stock Exchange as brokers unloaded stocks for their customers. The average stock lost more than 5 percent of its value during the day. The prices of more than 170 stocks dropped to their lowest level of the year. All told the value of stocks on the market fell by $4 billion.

The sell-off did not occur because investors had suddenly lost their confidence in the market and decided to bail out: most of those who sold did so because they were forced to. The margin game had finally caught up to a substantial group of small investors. During the past months the slide in stock market prices had eroded these margins. Whereas a couple of months ago investors could get away with paying for as little as 10 percent of their stock, now they had to come up with 75 percent. Many of these small investors had put all their savings into the market already and

Telephone operators at the New York Stock Exchange received a flurry of calls from customers rushing to sell their stocks on October 23, 1929.

did not have any more cash to meet the margin calls.

Others went even more deeply into debt by borrowing from banks to meet their margin calls. In many cases this strategy only compounded their problem. The banks required that the loans be secured by collateral. Collateral are the assets that a borrower pledges to give to the lender as compensation if, for any reason, the borrower cannot repay the loan. In 1929 many stock market investors used the value of their stock shares as collateral to get loans. For some, their investment bordered on a pyramid scheme—they pledged stock that they had bought on margin, and therefore did not re-

ally own, as collateral to get loans to buy more stock. Again, everything was fine as long as the stocks made money. If a person pledged $5,000 worth of stock to get a $5,000 loan, he had no problem as long as the market kept rising. But if the market fell and the value of the stocks dropped to $3,000, now the lender was in a risky position. Therefore, when values of stock collateral dropped, lenders required borrowers to come up with more collateral. If the borrowers could not do so, the stock had to be sold for what they could get for it.

In this latest market decline, brokers sold off enough stocks to reduce the total amount of their loans by over $167 million for the week. The selling spree and plummeting stock prices of Wednesday brought an edge of anxiety to the New York Stock Exchange. Most brokers still expected that the reduced prices would bring buyers flocking to the market on Thursday. But the possible consequences if that failed to happen were chilling enough that they could not rest easy until the rally actually began.

THURSDAY MORNING, OCTOBER 24

Early risers had a long and restless wait for the trading to begin on the morning of Thursday, October 24—the New York Stock Exchange did not open for its daily six-hour trading session until 10 A.M. Although the massive hall of the exchange contained over sixteen thousand square feet, the floor was crowded as every eligible trader was on duty. Whatever happened that day, officials expected the buying and selling to be fast and furious.

The New York Stock Exchange took pride in being the largest and most modernized stock exchange in the world. In order to facilitate the trading of over a thousand different stocks, eighteen posts were set up on the floor. Each company

Each company whose stock was traded on the large, modern New York Stock Exchange was assigned to one of eighteen posts on the floor.

trading on the exchange was assigned one of these posts where the buying or selling of its stocks would occur. For example, U.S. Steel traded at Post 2, RCA at Post 12. The entire floor had recently been carpeted to muffle the noise. Each transaction was recorded on ticker tape that ran continuously in broker offices around the nation during trading to provide up-to-the-moment prices to all participants. Roughly five hundred miles of tape spewed out of the tickers for every million shares traded, and the exchange averaged in the neighborhood of 3 to 4 million shares traded each day. On the exchange floor itself the roll of the ticker tape was magnified on giant screens for easy reading.

The floor was exceptionally quiet as the traders waited for the opening bell. Orderly and dignified behavior was expected of all traders on the floor. Exchange rules expressly forbid such actions as running, shouting, and cursing. But observers noticed something different about the calm that prevailed on this morning. This was the tense silence that hangs in the air the moment before the starting gun goes off in an important race.

As luck would have it, at this crucial juncture in the market, New York Stock Exchange president E. H. H. Simmons was thousands of miles away. He and his new wife had just traveled to Hawaii on their honeymoon. In his absence, vice president Richard Whitney would have to take charge for the next week.

Just before the market opened, market superintendent William Crawford was alerted to a call from Whitney. Tensions were so high that at first Crawford feared that Whitney had decided to close the exchange for the day in hopes of staving off a panic of selling. He was nearly giddy with relief when he learned that Whitney merely wanted to make him aware that Great Britain's famous politician, Winston Churchill, would be visiting the market at midmorning.

CAUGHT IN A VICIOUS CYCLE

As soon as the stock market opened the floor burst into activity. Stockbrokers armed with customer orders that had piled up in their offices since the close on Wednesday rushed to the trading posts to carry out their business. During the opening minutes the prices of some stocks jumped. But within minutes, the opening burst of buying fizzled out as a barrage of sell orders dragged prices down. Then stocks held steady for the next half hour. Brokers wiped their brows in relief that the market's fall appeared to have been stopped for the present.

By 10:45, however, optimism evaporated. The market was now being buried under a growing avalanche of orders to sell. Much of this selling was due to margin calls, which produced a vicious cycle of ever-increasing intensity. As stock prices lost their value, banks that had loaned money to brokers wanted their money back. Brokers had to retrieve the money from their investors. The only way for the many investors to come up with the money was to sell the stock. The more people were forced to sell their stocks, the fewer buyers existed for these stocks and therefore the lower the price would fall. The lower the price of the stocks, the greater the number of margin calls that went out and the greater the number of people who were forced to sell.

At this point another stock market mechanism kicked in to intensify the cycle. Many investors protected themselves against the possibility of a market collapse by giving their brokers "stop loss" orders. These were standing instructions to sell off the investors' stocks immediately if the price dropped to a certain level. The morning of the twenty-fourth, many stocks fell far enough to trigger stop loss orders. While these orders were intended to protect the investor from a stock market free fall, they only added to the catastrophe on Wall Street. Stop loss orders piled on top of the mountain of sell orders already burying the stock market created a massive oversupply of stocks on the market. This further fueled the plunge in prices.

On the other hand, some investment trusts had automatic buy orders in place to take swift advantage of brief dips in market prices. In this case, when the price of a stock dropped to a certain level, brokers were under orders to immediately buy that stock. Whether they wanted to or not, brokers had to honor these orders and ended up buying large blocks of stock that appeared to be certain to lose value almost as soon as they bought them.

STOCK MARKET CHAOS

As stock prices plummeted, stocks quickly became worthless as collateral for loans. This forced banks and other large investors to make an agonizing decision. Should they hang on to their stocks and even pur-chase more stock to avoid contributing to the panic-selling of stocks? Or should they dump their stocks now and get what they could from them before the market dropped even further? As Judith Baughman states, "The bankers were, in fact, in an impossible situation; to do what they knew should be done required them to act against their interests. Their instincts told them to sell, to get out from under as soon as possible."[23]

By eleven o'clock the mood of the stock exchange had deteriorated from anxiety to distress to fear and finally to panic. The volume of stocks being traded was almost beyond comprehension. Prices were dropping faster than most people believed possible. In such a crisis the long-standing rules on gentlemanly behavior fell by the wayside as brokers rushed from post to post, pushing through the crowds and shouting out their orders. Above the din on the stock market floor could be heard frantic shouts of "Sell at market!" One man, completely unnerved by falling stock values, yelled orders that made no sense until he was led away by friends.

In comparison with the previous day's record volume of 6 million shares, nearly 5 million shares were offered for sale in the first one-and-a-half hours of Thursday's trading. This volume so overwhelmed the ticker tape that it could not begin to keep up with the transactions. As a result many brokers had no idea what the latest price was on any given stock. Adding to the confusion was the fact that the telephone switchboards were tied up by thousands of people all trying to get in touch with their brokers or bankers. Away from the city the communication problem was even worse. With the ticker falling so far behind as to be worthless and the phone lines tied up, people in cities and towns all over the country searched frantically for news reports, rumors—anything to let them know what was happening. A severe ice storm that brought down telephone lines in the Midwest further compounded the confusion in that part of the nation.

The breakdown of communications put investors and brokers in a terrible situation. Given the way prices were falling, they re- alized that they could already be ruined by the time they got a clear picture of what was happening. The delay was especially hard on those people who had bought stocks on margin. Without accurate knowledge of exactly where prices were, they did not know whether they should put more money into the market to cover their losses or just default and avoid throwing good money after bad.

Lack of information produced fear that plunged the market into even greater chaos. Those investors in New York, who were

Brokers and investors across the country relied upon a ticker tape system for information about stock sales.

surrounded by wild-eyed traders desperate to unload stocks regardless of how low the market was at that moment, could hardly keep their imaginations from running rampant. Billions of dollars worth of stock investments were disappearing before their eyes. No one could get an accurate quote as to what price a given stock was worth. In such circumstances it took a person with nerves of steel to sit tight until the picture became clearer before taking action. Most were convinced that they had to act fast to avert utter ruin.

Meanwhile, across the nation, imaginations ran equally wild at the terrifying reports sputtering out of New York. Many investors guessed that their only hope of salvaging something out of this disaster was to sell and get what they could before prices collapsed to nothing. Even those whose stocks were actually weathering the storm in decent shape could not help but imagine that they were on the verge of being wiped out. More sell orders swamped the market, causing prices to collapse even further.

By 11:15 many brokers and investors were learning a painful but elementary lesson in economics: there could be no selling if there were no buyers. For the next hour or so traders found that they could not find any buyers at any price for numerous stocks. Even though interest rates on call money had dropped to their lowest levels of the year by midmorning, no one was interested in borrowing money to buy stocks in such a threatening environment. The decline of prices was truly astounding. By noon an estimated $6 to $8 billion out of a total market value of $80 billion had evap-

orated on the New York Stock Exchange. Judith Baughman summed up what was happening: "On this one business day—24 October 29—all the unthinkable crises and nightmares that had threatened during the preceding weeks came to pass."[24]

BANKS TO THE RESCUE

As the noon hour approached, none of the traders on the New York exchange dared to take even a few minutes off for lunch. Trading was so fast and furious that they could not afford to risk getting even further behind the situation than they already were. Spreading news of the catastrophe on the New York Stock Exchange had attracted crowds to Wall Street. The streets were jammed with brokers, worried investors, curious spectators, and reporters who had come to cover what was shaping up to be a major story.

The question on the minds of most veteran market observers was, "What are the big money interests going to do to stop the disaster?" In past stock market crashes, wealthy investors had taken bold steps to pour their vast resources into the market to create enough demand to soak up the surplus of sell orders. Most memorably, legendary banker J. P. Morgan had organized the pillars of the financial community to help put the brakes on the panic of 1907.

At noon the financial giants began to move. New York Stock Exchange vice president Whitney closed the public gallery in an effort to restore some order to the exchange. Then he met with twenty of the nation's most influential bankers, who together were worth an estimated $6 billion,

MORGAN TO THE RESCUE

The reason the bankers' intervention was so highly anticipated on October 24 was because of how a powerful group of investors, led by legendary banker J. P. Morgan, had saved the nation from a similar disaster in 1907. In Morgan: American Financier, *Jean Strouse quotes an admirer of Morgan as telling a friend:*

"[Morgan's] position today in America is not due to his riches. There are 20 richer men there. It is due to the fact that in the dark days of 1907, he knew no fear, he believed in the country and himself and imparted pluck and spirit to others and infused strength and hope into men 20, 30, and 40 years younger than himself. If he had given way, the whole house of financial cards would have fallen."

J.P. Morgan

in a closed session across the street from the stock exchange in the offices of the J. P. Morgan bank.

The news that such men were meeting was enough to temporarily brake the momentum of the stock decline. Even in the face of disaster the public regarded these financial wizards with awe and had confidence that they would soon set things right. Stock prices not only stopped their free fall but actually inched forward as everyone waited to hear what actions the group would take.

Whitney emerged from the brief meeting as the group's representative, entrusted with a staggering amount of investment money. At 1:15 he arrived at the stock market floor, aware that all eyes were on him. Oozing confidence in his impeccably tailored suit, he made his way through the crowd milling about Post 2 and in a loud voice asked for the latest price of U.S. Steel. This bastion of the stock market had begun the day at $245 a share, but had tumbled all the way down to $195. Whitney could easily have purchased the stock for that price, but he wanted to make a dramatic statement to reassure investors that the big investors were actively supporting the market. He offered to buy twenty-five thousand shares at $205 a share.

New York Stock Exchange vice president Richard Whitney secured an estimated $30 million from America's top bankers in an effort to restore investor confidence in the stock market.

The crowd greeted his offer with cheers and shouts of relief. Whitney then went around to other posts, buying large blocks of high-profile stocks such as General Motors and AT&T. All told, Whitney invested an estimated $30 million of the bankers' money.

Whitney's dramatic and conspicuous gesture appeared to achieve the desired effect of restoring confidence in the stock market. During the afternoon many stocks began climbing in price. Some would even finish the day higher than when it started. Most of the crowd milling along Wall Street was convinced that the big money people had saved the day and that the great rally had begun.

Chapter

5 The Bottom Falls Out

While spectators and stock traders were hailing the start of the rally on Thursday afternoon, investors and brokers around the nation were reacting quite differently. For them the ticker tape was the only reliable source of information about what was happening at the New York Stock Exchange. It alone could tell them whether they were still financially solvent or had just lost their entire life savings, and they watched it throughout the day as though mesmerized.

Unfortunately the ticker tape was overwhelmed by an unimaginable record volume of 12.9 million shares traded. The ticker tape did not catch up with sales until four hours after closing. All stock market employees were required to stay late to clear up the backlog and sort out all the paperwork. Some of them would be unable to go home for days.

This simple technology failure contributed greatly to the chaos in the stock market. The ticker tape's failure to give customers timely information created a completely misleading impression of events. The tape had fallen so far behind that all the out-of-town folks saw throughout the afternoon was the relentless drop in prices from the morning's activity. At the very time when the bankers' public show of support was

starting to reestablish some trust on Wall Street, spurring a rally, investors and brokers across the nation were still reeling under the

The record volume of shares traded during the crash overwhelmed the ticker tape system.

shock of a disaster that appeared to have no end in sight. Hundreds of thousands of people had no idea whether they had any savings or not. Many of them decided that they had no choice but to salvage what little they could by getting out of the stock market as fast as possible. Sell orders mounted even during the afternoon rally. The New York activity also had an adverse effect on other stock exchanges. Trading at both the Chicago and San Francisco stock exchanges grew so frantic that they closed early to prevent panic selling.

CAUTIOUS OPTIMISM

Optimism had never been in short supply on Wall Street during the 1920s, and even in the face of Thursday's scare many people confidently predicted that the worst

was over. After all, by closing time some of the highest profile stocks, such as U.S. Steel, had rebounded to near their starting levels of the day. The Dow Jones average ended the day down only slightly and had been rising at closing time. News reports from Wall Street played up the bankers' dramatic intervention and the market's subsequent recovery.

Many Wall Street experts believed that Thursday's frightening roller-coaster ride might even have been a good thing. For example, the tremendous sales volume had been a windfall for stockbrokers. Since they received a commission on sales, Thursday's trading had brought in nearly twice as much commission money as any previous day on Wall Street.

The sudden plunge in prices, the experts said, was a natural correction of a situation in which too many uninformed people had

---

FALSE OPTIMISM

Wall Street's boldest investors continued to totally misjudge the stock market situation right up to the last minute. On October 28, the night before he was to lose his entire multimillion-dollar fortune, Herbert Swope viewed the situation as follows, quoted in Grant's Bernard Baruch: The Adventures of a Wall Street Legend:

"Think I am able to see change in situation for better so am making determined effort to hold on stocks believe you should too. Consensus of opinion of meeting at Baruch's . . . was that those who stand pressure would not alone be discharging public duty but would be conferring by favor upon themselves with certainty of recovery of stocks whose values undoubtedly far greater than today's market regardless of high or low quotation in past. . . . I discovered distinct change for better tonight in that men were talking again about making money instead of merely losing money."

President Herbert Hoover assured the country that the stock market plunge of October 24 was a healthy adjustment in response to widespread margin speculation.

been speculating with money they did not have. Those people panicked and sold. Most of those who remained were wealthier investors who had resisted the pressures to sell. The market would be well rid of the amateurs and behave more rationally now that the bulk of investors were people with sound financial resources who had a good understanding of how the market worked. They would be less likely to panic and take actions that would send the stock market plummeting again. Those smart small investors who had survived the market scare of Thursday could be expected to follow the lead of the wealthy investors and pick up some of the hardest-hit stocks at bargain prices.

On Friday morning a crowd of spectators gathered around the New York Stock Exchange. The crowd cheered employees of J. P. Morgan as they arrived at their offices near the stock exchange, convinced that the bankers had saved their fortunes. They awaited the start of trading fully believing that they had survived the worst scare the stock market could throw at them, and that this would be a profitable day for the market.

Government officials agreed with this sentiment. President Hoover declared to the nation that day, "The fundamental business of the country, that is, the production and the distribution of commodities, is on a sound and prosperous basis."[25] His administration characterized Thursday's bizarre events as a healthy and long overdue resolution to an unhealthy situation of overspeculation, and assured the people that there was no cause for alarm and certainly none for government intervention.

Friday's trading on the New York Stock Exchange seemed to justify the prevailing optimism. Trading was far more subdued, with a far more manageable 6 million shares being traded, and stock prices rose slightly. In relatively light trading on the half-day Saturday trading session, prices remained fairly stable. Top financial men such as Charlie Mitchell declared that everything was back to normal.

WEEKEND REFLECTION

Despite the optimism, the weekend cast a shadow of mystery over the stock market. The stock markets were not open on Sundays and this gave investors a chance to catch their breath and reflect on Thursday's scare. There was no way to determine what they were thinking or discussing among their friends and advisers. People such as Whitney recognized there was a chance that rumors and fears could be spreading during this down period and that these could spark another nervous sell-off on Monday. Yet as Monday approached, the mood of the New York stock market was upbeat. Many observers expected the market to follow past form and that the sputtering rally would reignite. Word on the street was that investors, having come to their senses after the near-disaster of Thursday, were now rushing to take advantage of bargain prices. There were even reports that brokers' offices were filled with piles of buy orders from around the nation and that this demand would unleash a tremendous rally on Monday.

In fact, however, fear was at work, gnawing at the wills of investors over the weekend. The most critical effect of the Thursday disaster was that it popped the bubble of invincibility in which the stock market had been floating for years. Investors who had formerly considered the stock market a surefire investment had, for the first time, come face-to-face with the terrifying possibility that they could lose their entire fortunes if another such run occurred. Many of them had seen it happen to their friends and acquaintances on Thursday. As they pondered the emotions of that day, they decided that they did not have the stomach for gambling their financial security on such a risky proposition as the stock market.

For those with time to reflect, other ominous signs were appearing on the economic horizon. Thursday's panic on Wall Street had created a ripple effect throughout much of the economy. Wheat prices had dropped ten cents a bushel that day, the most severe price drop in the U.S. grain market's history. Thousands of people had lost their savings during the margin calls and sell-offs that day. Even corporations such as General Motors looked around and saw trouble coming. On that Thursday its management began planning for the likelihood of an economic recession in coming weeks. On Friday an estimated two hundred thousand people lost their jobs nationwide, partly as a consequence of the economic damage from Thursday's losses. That same day a substantial number of out-of-town bankers began pulling money out of the New York exchange, looking for more secure investments.

The fear and uncertainty that took hold of investors over the weekend put them in a different mood than had been the case before Thursday. Whereas before they were reluctant to sell stocks for fear of losing out on a chance for even more spectacular gains, now they were looking for any opportunity to sell. When prices rebounded to respectable levels late in the previous week, many decided to take advantage of the fact and sell out before the market took another tumble.

MONDAY SURPRISE

So many people came to that same conclusion that, when added to the weakened demand caused by departure of margin investors who had been sold out, the result was an unexpected, relentless selling spree on Monday. Prices spiraled downward all day, wiping out in a few hours all the gains made in the brief Thursday afternoon–Friday rally. The decline was more orderly this time. For the most part it was wealthier, veteran stock market investors who took

the hit, and they did not panic as readily as the investors had Tuesday in the mass confusion that surrounded the market.

But neither were there any deep-pocketed bankers rushing to the rescue as they had on Thursday. Although the $30 million that Whitney had pumped into the market that day had seemed like a substantial amount, it was but a drop in the bucket compared to the values of the stocks. The bankers' action was more of a bluff than a remedy. Its importance had been as a symbolic gesture to boost the confidence of investors. This latest selling spree was evidence that its success had been very short-lived. There was no point in trying to bluff a second time when the first one

Although these stock clerks seem cheerful, a massive stock sell-off sent the stock market into a rapid downward spiral on October 28.

had already been called. Furthermore, many of the largest investors were firm believers in the power of the marketplace to regulate itself. Supply and demand was the best way of determining values, they believed, and attempts to manipulate it were futile. They decided to let the stock prices fall and trusted the laws of supply and demand to stabilize the situation.

The stock sell-off dragged the market down steadily throughout the day. Virtually no stock was immune, as even favorites such as U.S. Steel and General Electric plummeted. As stock values evaporated, the cycle of margin calls and defaults kicked in again. Eventually the relentless downward pressures cracked even prudent and prosperous investors. Those who had the resources to withstand margin calls the previous week now found that they had to come up with yet more money to save their investments. Lenders began to sweat as they realized that even their largest customers were having trouble covering their margins or producing the needed collateral. Some lenders had so much money loaned out to their best clients that a default on those loans would ruin the bank. They had no choice but to order the brokers holding these loans to sell huge blocks of stock at whatever they could get for them rather than risk losing everything in a market crash.

By the end of the day, fear gripped even veteran Wall Street investors, and they began to wonder if this would be their last chance to escape before the market collapsed and they lost all their money. In the final hour of trading on Monday the exchange degenerated into the frantic scene that had taken hold early on Thursday. An incredible 3 million shares were thrown out for sale in that time, and prices were nearly in a free fall by the time the market closed—well below the Thursday levels. On average, stocks on the exchange finished the day worth less than 90 per cent of their value when the day started.

PANIC!

One of the few eyewitness accounts of the stock market trading on October 29 came from Richard Whitney, quoted in The Day the Bubble Burst, *by Thomas and Morgan-Witts:*

"Panic was raging overhead on the floor. Every few minutes the latest prices were announced, with quotations moving swiftly and irresistibly downward. The feeling of those present was revealed by their habit of continually lighting cigarettes, taking a puff or two, putting them out and lighting new ones—a practice that soon made the narrow room blue with smoke and extremely stuffy."

DESPAIR ON WALL STREET

By Tuesday morning the last pockets of optimism had been burst by dread of a market collapse. Even the most rock-solid stock market customers, the large institutions, found themselves caught in a bind. The institutional investors were not speculators. They did not borrow money to purchase stock. By and large they invested their own funds in solid companies' stocks and held them for a long period of time, collecting dividends from the profits of these companies. As such they were not greatly affected by the day-to-day fluctuations of the market, nor were they affected by margin calls. But their investment managers realized that a total market collapse would reduce the value of their stocks to almost nothing. They could not just sit by and watch the millions of dollars entrusted to their safekeeping dwindle away. Since they had held their stocks for a long time, most were still worth a good deal more than they had paid for them, even in the plummeting market. Better to get out now, they figured, than to risk losing everything. Overnight thousands of sell orders from large institutions piled up in the offices of stockbrokers.

Thousands of investors gathered on Wall Street on the morning of Tuesday, October 29. The New York Stock Exchange gallery was still closed to spectators, but with so much at stake on this day, people wanted to be close to the action, to find out as soon as possible what their futures would hold.

As William Crawford lowered the gavel to start Tuesday's trading, a thunderous roar erupted from the traders. Huge chunks of stock in the United States' most celebrated

On October 29 Wall Street was filled with thousands of investors clamoring for news.

companies were offered for sale. Within three minutes, 650,000 shares of U.S. Steel stock were dumped on the market. In the first thirty minutes of trading, stocks on the New York Stock Exchange lost over $2 billion in value as more than 3 million shares were put up for sale.

TOTAL CHAOS

Still, the damage was not as bad as many people had feared. Some stocks, such as Woolworth, withstood the sell-off and stubbornly held their value. For a few brief minutes there was hope that the great catastrophe that investors feared would not come to pass. But the flood of sell orders kept coming. With so many people wanting to sell and so few wanting to buy, the decline of prices began accelerating. U.S. Steel, which had sold for $245 a share less than a week earlier, crashed through the $200 level to $179. RCA, once known as a glamour stock that had rewarded investors with fabulous wealth, dropped $10 a share in the opening minutes and kept falling.

As stock prices plunged, some brokers lost their nerve and panic-selling accelerated. Again, the ticker tape fell so far behind the transactions that it was almost impossible to determine what a specific stock was worth at any particular time. The floor of the exchange degenerated into total chaos with shouts of "Sell at market!" echoing from every trading post. A *London News* reporter described the traders as a "leaderless and panic-stricken mob." As an example of how quickly a fortune could vanish in such an environment, a company called Blue Ride Corporation opened the day selling for $110 a share. Before the day was out it was selling for $3 a share, and even at that, those trying to sell could not find a buyer. Union Cigar went into a similar free fall, opening the day at $113.50 a share and finishing at $4. Under such conditions even the largest, most patient, and most optimistic investors who had been resolutely

waiting out the storm finally threw in the towel. Better to get something out of the investment before it became completely worthless, they believed. With every person who gave up and sold even at these deflated prices, the values of stocks spiraled lower.

In just two hours, 8 million shares had been thrown on the market. This was 2 million more shares than had ever been traded in a full day up until a week before. Even U.S. Steel was falling into uncharted areas—dropping below $170 a share and still sinking.

In the early afternoon the New York Stock Exchange Board convened an emergency meeting to deal with the situation. Some members wanted to close the stock market until the wave of panic had subsided. But Whitney and others worried that, given the current chaotic situation, if the market closed it might never open again. After much discussion the board decided to stay open and hope that things somehow would improve.

BLACK TUESDAY

Outside the exchange, confusion reigned as well. By early afternoon Wall Street was gridlocked with ten thousand people all straining to catch some word of how their stocks were doing. Solid information was hard to come by and rumors flew through the air. No one knew what to believe. But the one common thread in all the reports filtering out of the exchange was that the damage was horrific. As the magnitude of the disaster set in, the crowd walked around in a daze. People cried openly. Nearby churches filled with stunned and despairing investors seeking some glimmer of hope in their ruined lives.

At about 2:30 P.M. the free fall in prices finally stopped. There was even a weak rally in the last half hour as a few brave investors could not resist picking up some of the choicest stocks at half of what they had sold for a week earlier. But this late activity could not begin to repair the damage. When the dust cleared from the day's activity, traders were left to pick up the pieces of the worst day in stock market history—a day forever known on Wall Street as "Black Tuesday." On average, New York exchange stocks lost more than 13 percent of their value in a single day. This translated into losses for investors of more than $9 billion. Combined with equally astounding losses in the other stock exchanges around the nation, more than $15 billion disappeared in a single day. This was roughly twice as much as all the currency in circulation in the United States at that time and about ten times the Union budget during the entire U.S. Civil War.

Combined with the batterings the market had taken on Monday and the past Thursday, the damage was even more catastrophic. Virtually every stock was currently worth considerably less than it had been a year earlier. The thirty leading industrial stocks had lost an average of 40 percent of their value since the high-water mark of September 3. This translated to anywhere from $30 to $50 billion worth of stock values disappearing from the economy in less than two months.

MOB PSYCHOLOGY

In 1936, banker J. M. Barker described how the stock market crash affected the business world, quoted in The Hungry Years, *by Watkins:*

"If you consider the universality of the speculative mania of the later days of the last boom, you will see how completely the people of the country, to say nothing of the world, were under the influence of the mob psychology of unreasoning, emotional cupidity [greed]. When the break came, cupidity turned into unreasoning, emotional fear. . . . In every city of the country, businessmen, hard hit or already wiped out in the stock market in the earlier part of the crash, were still watching the quotations every day to see how things were going. They saw the market dropping, dropping, dropping. Is there any doubt they made their decisions from day to day under the influence of the emotional backgrounds formed by their observations of the falling security prices?"

THE AFTERMATH

On Wednesday the panic was over, replaced by a stunned and listless resignation. Any hope for a significant rally was dashed when many of the nation's top banks and investors recalled over $2 billion in loans that had been financing stock purchases. Even though interest rates charged for stock loan money were more than twice what they had been a year earlier, upwards of 12 percent, the banks did not consider the possible gains worth the risk of lending money in the market.

Stocks staged a half-hearted rally on Wednesday, but not enough to even put a bandage on the massive wound the market had suffered. Traders were still floundering under the mountain of paperwork that had accumulated from the incredible 16,388,700 shares traded on Black Tuesday. The New York Stock Exchange Board declared a suspension of trading on Friday and Saturday to let its members catch up.

So many stocks were exchanged on "Black Tuesday" that trading in New York was suspended for two days later in the week to allow traders across the country to catch up with paperwork.

ROCKEFELLER'S REASSURANCE

For a brief time on October 30 stock prices advanced following this announcement by the reclusive John D. Rockefeller, the world's richest man, quoted in The Day America Crashed, *by Tom Shachtman:*

"These are the days when many are discouraged. . . . In the ninety years of my life, depressions have come and gone. Prosperity has always returned, and will come again. . . . Believing that the fundamental conditions of the country are sound, my sons and I have been purchasing sound common stocks for some days."

John D. Rockefeller (center) and his son, (left).

When it reopened, the market showed no more signs of life than it had before. On November 4, average prices sank even lower. Some of the nation's wealthiest business leaders continued their attempts to rally discouraged investors by arguing that the stock market collapse was strictly a result of panic and did not reflect true economic or investment conditions. Even John D. Rockefeller, the richest man in the world and a person who had doggedly avoided the public spotlight for most of his long life, came to the stock market's defense. He issued this statement: "Believing that the fundamental conditions of the country are sound, my sons and I have been purchasing sound common stocks for some days."[26] But that news was greeted with indifference or outright scorn. Comedian Eddie Cantor drew laughs from his embittered audience by asking, "Sure, who else has money?"[27]

Confidence in the stock market had been shattered and there was nothing Rockefeller or anyone else could do to restore it. Even investors who scooped up stocks at these incredibly low prices quickly unloaded them as soon as the prices went up, causing the price to fall back and stifling any possible prolonged rally. Stock prices continued to slide until they reached their low point on November 13. Even the most solid companies in the United States suffered disastrous losses. U.S. Steel, which had sold for $261 a share on September 3, fell to $150 per share by mid-November. General Electric, considered a good buy at $396 a share in September, plummeted to $168. RCA, one of the fastest-rising stocks in the land during the late 1920s, crashed from $101 a share on September 3 to $28 on November 13.

Once the shock wore off, it became obvious that there was no quick and easy way to counteract or reverse the stock market crash. The crash was a fact of life and the only questions that remained were how long would it last, how would it affect the nation, and how was the country going to go about recovering from it.

6 Immediate Effect of the Crash on Americans

The stock market crash of 1929 bankrupted more investors by far than all the nation's previous economic panics combined. The most conspicuous victims of the stock market crash were the rich. In the last months of 1929 the same newspapers that had trumpeted the spectacular rise to fortune of high-stakes stock market investors were now filled with dramatic stories of America's financial elite falling into ruin.

HIGH-PROFILE VICTIMS OF THE CRASH

Multimillionaires who had been in a position to live out their lives in luxury without having to work another day suddenly found themselves penniless. Included in this group were professional investors who had boasted of reputations as some of the shrewdest money manipulators in the market. Will Durant, who some said had made more money in the 1920s bull market than anyone else, was one of these. Jesse Livermore, one of the most celebrated Wall Street traders in history, lost his multimillion-dollar fortune by betting heavily that the market would make a quick recovery. A business tycoon named Edward Stone watched his $5 million for-

tune evaporate in a few hours. Another, newspaper editor Herbert Swope, had been sitting on a $14 million nest egg on Labor Day; by Thanksgiving he was $2 million in debt. The dollar figures are especially mind-boggling considering that a dollar then was

The American media reported the ruin of many wealthy individual investors.

---

worth several times more than one today.

One of the biggest losers in the crash was Michael Meehan, a stockbroker who had gained fame by accumulating a fortune in stocks, especially RCA. Although Meehan lost an estimated $40 million in the crash, he was luckier than most—he still had $20 million to fall back on.

Not only did wealthy individual investors take devastating hits, but investment firms found themselves in deep trouble. Nearly every one of the 751 investment trusts operating at the New York Stock Exchange was fatally wounded by the events of October 29. By mid-November some of the largest and most reputable investment firms in New York declared bankruptcy.

The stock market crash rocked some of the nation's major lenders to the core. Among these was the Union Industrial Bank of Flint, Michigan. For about a year a group of managers at the bank had secretly been using some of the bank's assets to invest in the stock market. Having faith that the stock market was a no-lose proposition, they rationalized that they could make a quick killing on stocks and replace the money with no one the wiser. Instead, when the market began to drop in September, their investments lost money. The schemers had no choice but to invest more of their customers' savings in their secret accounts to meet margin calls. When the bottom dropped out on October 29, most of that money evaporated. The anguished conspirators finally had to confess to bank president Charles Stewart Mott that they had illegally squandered over $3.5 million from the bank's savings accounts. Since the embezzlers were broke, Mott, a wealthy man, tried to make up the difference from his own savings. Nonetheless, some Union Industrial customers never did get their money back.

UNDERESTIMATING THE CRASH

On November 6, 1929, even Bernard Baruch, who had saved his fortune by exercising doubts about the stability of the stock market prior to the crash, did not understand the seriousness of the economic situation. Quoted in Bernard Baruch: The Adventures of a Wall Street Legend, *by Grant:*

"Looks like all technical and forced liquidation about completed. Only thing unpleasant in sight is present and prospective decline in business which will be bad but will be much exaggerated as the bullish was overexaggerated six months ago. How hysterical business men will now become regarding business you can judge as well as anyone but business cannot remain very bad in this country long."

High-profile entertainers like Groucho Marx lost sizable savings in the crash.

Also, well-known amateur investors such as the popular Marx Brothers comedy team and composer Irving Berlin suffered horrendous losses. Upon the advice of financial professionals, they had invested their hefty earnings in the stock market. Groucho Marx was persuaded that buying on margin was the fastest way to make money in the stock market, and he did so even though he had plenty of savings to buy the stocks outright. When the stock market fell and his lenders repeatedly asked

him to come up with the money to cover the margins, he had the financial resources to do so. Eventually though, his stocks' value evaporated until Marx's entire savings of $250,000 was wiped out.

JUMPING OUT OF WINDOWS

One wealthy widow shrugged off the loss of her $1 million fortune by declaring that she had enjoyed every minute of her exhilarating

MOOD OF DEFEAT

"It was a year of suicides, not only among stockbrokers but also among wealthy dilettantes. It was a year when faces looked white and nervous; a year on insomnia and sleeping tablets. It was a year when classmates and former friends became involved in speakeasy brawls, divorces, defalcations [embezzlements] and even murders; the underworld and the upper world were close to each other. Most of all it was a year when a new mood became perceptible, a mood of doubt and even defeat. People began to wonder whether it wasn't possible that not only their ideas but their whole lives had been set in the wrong direction."

Wall Street ride. Most well-off investors, however, found it difficult to cope with the shock of losing their fortunes. One of the most enduring images of the 1929 stock market crash is that of distraught brokers and investors jumping to their deaths from Manhattan skyscraper windows. According to rumors of the time, and legends that have persisted, dozens of once-affluent people committed suicide in this way rather than face the shame of huge debts and of bringing clients to ruin with their advice.

There were, indeed, cases of men and women who killed themselves in despondency over their losses. One of the most prominent was Jim Riordan, president of County Trust Company, who shot himself on November 8 when his financial losses brought him to the point of despair. Also, a few people did end their lives by leaping out of windows; Winston Churchill reported witnessing one such incident on his visit to Wall Street on October 24.

Scattered incidents such as these led to rumors of an epidemic of window-jumpings. On Black Tuesday, however, an ambulance responding to reports of such activity slowly wormed its way through the thick crowds milling on Wall Street only to find that no one had jumped. Unfortunately, a British newspaper reporter accepted the rumors without verifying them. He cabled a report to his home office that Manhattan was littered with bodies of those who had leaped out of windows. The report worked its way into worldwide presses without being challenged. Humorist Will Rogers then forever cemented the myth on November 10, 1932, when he quipped, "The situation has been reached in New York hotels where the clerk asks incoming guests, 'You wanna room for sleeping or for jumping? And you have to stand in line to get a window to jump out of.'"[28] In reality, neither national statistics nor those limited to New York showed any significant increase in suicides during the autumn of 1929.

LOW-PROFILE VICTIMS

While the spectacular losses of the rich drew the most attention, the vast majority of those hurt in the stock market crash were middle-class Americans. Of the 125 million people living in the United States in 1929, an estimated 15 to 25 million were either stockholders or family members of stockholders. Few of these people had funds in reserve. Many had worked hard all of their lives to save a meager amount and viewed the stock market as their only chance to achieve some sort of financial security. Since so many of them were able to enter the stock market only by buying on margin,

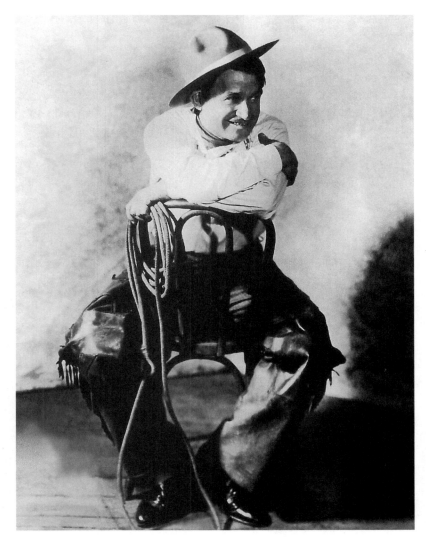

A Will Rogers quip perpetuated the myth that countless people facing financial ruin in the crash had jumped to their deaths from New York City windows.

they were the hardest hit when margin calls came and they were unable to come up with the funds. Millions of middle-class and even working-class Americans lost all their savings—every cent they had saved from years of hard work and sacrifice. With no money put away for retirement and with a limited number of earning years left at low wages, the future looked grim for them. Many spent the rest of their days trying to earn enough just to scrape by from day to day.

THE WINNERS

However, a few individuals were able to profit from even so great a disaster as the stock market crash. Foremost among these was Roger Babson, the economist whose prediction of a catastrophic crash had been widely publicized. When the crash took place, Babson gained a reputation as a financial genius. In the following years he gained a wide following among those still brave enough to invest money in the stock market.

For the small number of investors who had had the foresight, or the luck, to withdraw their money from the stock market just before the crash hit, the depressed market was a great opportunity. Some over-eager exploiters such as Jesse Livermore were badly burned by getting back into the market too aggressively before it hit bottom. But those who cautiously searched for bargains among the rubble of the battered stocks ended up in great shape. Bernard Baruch and Joseph Kennedy, who had been convinced that stock prices were artificially high in September, now recognized that some good stocks were artificially devalued simply because of panic selling. The key to success was patience. They waited until market prices bottomed out, then picked up thousands of cheap shares of stock in financially sound companies and patiently held on to them during the many months when

SERIOUS FAILURE OF BUSINESS

Quoted in FDR: A Biography, *by Ted Morgan, Franklin Roosevelt illustrates the loss of credibility suffered by the U.S. business community:*

"Many of the so-called businessmen and financiers, even now, after two years of depression, have not the foggiest idea of what happened. . . . As to the suggestion that `the great silent body of American people' believe that any . . . minor regulation of business by the government has been responsible for our troubles, I am inclined to think that the contrary is true. Most average citizens with whom I talk are impressed with the rather serious failure of business to prevent conditions when they had a chance to do so."

the market seemed to be going nowhere. Eventually, after several years, these shares regained their value.

MAJORITY OF AMERICANS UNAFFECTED

For the majority of Americans, the 100 million or so whose families owned no stock, the Wall Street panic had no immediate impact. Except for those who personally knew someone who had lost everything in the crash, most viewed the despairing headlines coming from New York as detached spectators. In fact, in towns, cities, and farms throughout the nation, most people thought that the stock market's stumble was greatly overpublicized—an example of journalists trying to create a sensational story out of nothing. They did not see how the fact that wealthy investors living a thousand miles away had lost money would affect their lives. From their perspective the crash was basically a case of rich people gambling and scheming and then finally getting the comeuppance they deserved.

In the weeks following the debacle, factories were still operating, stores remained open, and workers reported to their jobs as usual. Industries continued to expand and the construction trades kept on building. As far as average people could see, nothing in their lives had changed. According to Judith Baughman, "For the most part, ordinary Americans looked forward to the new decade with confidence in the economy."[29]

GOVERNMENT REACTION

The federal government, although concerned about the effects of such a large loss of money by major financial institutions, held much the same view. On December 13, in his annual report to Congress on the state of the nation, President Hoover tried to reassure Americans by declaring that the economy was basically sound. Some federal officials went so far as to say that the crash was a good thing. The reckless speculation and wildly fluctuating market conditions had created a very unstable business climate. The stock market crash was a stiff dose of corrective medicine that returned sanity to the market.

While conceding that some individuals were badly hurt, the government believed that the effects of the crash on the economy would be minor and short-term. At the end of November, government financial experts estimated that the stock market would recover in two to three months. A few weeks later the U.S. Department of Labor predicted that 1930 would be an excellent year for employment. Secretary of the Treasury Andrew Mellon greeted the new year in January with a declaration that the nation would see steady economic growth in 1930.

"I see nothing in the present situation that is either menacing or warrants pessimism," he said. "During the winter months there may be some slackness or unemployment, but hardly more than at this season each year."[30]

The most decisive response to the crash taken by any government official on any

Continuation of work on the Empire State Building in Manhattan was an optimistic sign in the wake of the stock market collapse.

level was New York City mayor Jimmy Walker's directive that theaters should show cheerful movies to lighten the mood of depressed investors.

FINANCIAL COMMUNITY REACTION

For the most part, business analysts agreed with the government and the common citi-

zens that the stock market crash was a minor setback. They concurred with the government's assessment of a quick recovery. One of the most optimistic signs that business was shrugging off the setback was the progress being made on the most ambitious building project in history, New York City's Empire State Building. Although John Jacob Raskob, the prime financial force behind the creation of what would be the world's tallest structure, suffered stiff losses in the stock market decline, the project moved forward as scheduled right in the heart of Manhattan, the site of the stock market disaster.

FUNDAMENTAL CHANGES

The average American, the government, and the business community all badly underestimated the effects of the stock market crash. Two immediate effects of the disaster proved to be irreversible: a change in attitudes of Americans regarding the business community, and the domino effect of the crash on the economy.

Although wealthy individuals and professional investors who still had money after the crash eventually returned to the market to buy devalued stocks, the small investors did not. Many of them had no choice; they had lost all their money and had nothing left to invest. But even those who had escaped with part of their savings intact looked at the stock market far differently than they had in previous years. Having been burned badly once, they were not about to venture into that arena again. As millions of investors dropped out of the market for good, there was no way that the demand for stocks could even approach its previous levels. With demand low, stock market prices could not rise.

Furthermore, the unexpected jolt of the 1929 crash changed the way Americans viewed the business community. Whereas before, high-stakes financial wizards were the heroes of the age, now they had become the villains. They were seen as the agents of ruin who had led so many naive small investors to disaster with their false promises of riches. The public turned with

FALL OF A FINANCIAL WIZARD

William C. Durant suffered the fate of falling from a net worth of many millions of dollars to deep debt that forced him to file this humiliating court action, quoted in The Dream Maker: William C. Durant, Founder of GM, *by Bernard Weisberger:*

"My petition in bankruptcy, filed today, is due to frequent and repeated court proceedings instituted by a few creditors, representing less than 5 percent of my total obligations, who have attempted to obtain a preferential position.

Action by creditors referred to have prevented me from giving my best efforts to rebuilding my fortune, and I no longer propose to be harassed and annoyed. I wish to state that all creditors will be treated alike, and if fortune favors me all will be paid in full."

a vengeance on people such as Stock Exchange vice president Richard Whitney and banker Charles Mitchell. Whitney was eventually convicted of illegal inside trading and spent time in prison, while Mitchell paid a stiff fine for tax evasion. Wall Street became a synonym for crooks and thieves.

SUSPICION OF THE BANKS

The new wave of suspicion against business interests counteracted the new and effective techniques of advertising that had held many ordinary Americans in its spell and lured them into believing in the infal-

After the 1929 crash, Americans began to vilify financial magnates like Richard Whitney, who later served a prison sentence for inside trading.

libility of the free market. Some of this suspicion was transferred to banks.

Not all lenders had been able to secure enough collateral or margin money to cover the loans before falling stock prices ruined the borrowers. Even banks that had avoided lending to stock market speculators got caught in a bind. They had extended credit to formerly reliable customers for traditional loan purchases such as homes and cars. When these people lost all of their savings in the stock market crash and could not repay the loans, the banks got stuck with the bad debts. Some of them could not recover from these losses and when they went out of business, they took their depositors' money down the drain with them. With every bank that failed, the newly wary customers of surviving banks grew more concerned about their savings accounts. In view of recent events, many came to the conclusion that the only safe place for their money was in their homes where they could see it.

Again, a vicious cycle was started. Mass withdrawal of funds by customers, known as a "run on the bank," could cause a bank to fail. Every failure made depositors more nervous about the safety of their money and led to more withdrawals, which in turn led to more bank failures. Bank failures were not concentrated on Wall Street. Banks throughout the nation, even in rural areas where little stock market speculating had taken place, suffered the same loss of confidence.

DISAPPEARING DEMAND FOR PRODUCTS

At the same time that the banks were struggling, U.S. industry began losing its already shaky footing. Prior to the crash, many factories had produced far more goods than the nation's consumers could buy. This situation was aggravated by the losses of the crash. A substantial portion of the population, suddenly with far less money to spend than just a few weeks before, had to cut back considerably on spending, further reducing the demand for goods. Thousands could not afford to pay for what they had already purchased on credit. Installment plan purchases that had been the rage suddenly fell out of favor. Consumers, sobered by the fate of overextended investors, steered away from taking on debt to make purchases. Lenders, burned by a large number of loan defaults, became very careful about making further loans.

The drop in demand for consumer products struck the automobile industry particularly hard. Manufacturers and dealers saw sales plummet just as their inventories were bursting at the seams. Demand for cars dropped so low that Ford had no choice but to reduce its prices drastically, and still car dealers had trouble selling their products.

Congress then compounded the problem of slow demand. In its effort to protect U.S. manufacturers from foreign competition, it passed a highly restrictive tariff on imports. This raised the price of imported goods, which made them less competitive against American-made products. The countries exporting these products to the United States reacted angrily to the tariff by imposing retaliatory tariffs of their own on goods imported from the United States This made U.S. products unaffordable overseas and eliminated markets that overstocked American corporations desperately needed.

Domino Effect on the U.S. Economy

Government and business analysts badly misjudged the effects that such a huge loss of capital combined with the nation's other economic problems would have on the U.S. economy. Industrial production in the country fell by 7 percent in November. December saw the private construction business shrink by 43 percent compared to the previous month. The stock market crash precipitated a panic in the grain exchanges that caused grain prices to sink even lower, sending already strapped farmers into unmanageable debt. With all this going on, the nation was sliding relentlessly into a situation that few could have imagined in the heady years of the Roaring Twenties. As historian Tom Shachtman observed, "Everything in the life of the country had changed. It would henceforth never be the same."[31]

7 Long-Term Effects of the Stock Market Crash

Periods of difficult economic conditions, known either as depressions or recessions depending on the severity of the problems, were nothing new to the U.S. business community in 1929. These periods had come with disheartening frequency and for a variety of reasons ever since the birth of the nation. In the past three decades alone there had been three such periods, in 1904, 1907, and 1921. All of these, however, had been brief, lasting a little over a year. The most severe depressions, such as those that occurred in 1837 and 1893, lasted nearly four years.

Estimates of exactly how long the Great Depression beginning in 1929 lasted vary with historians. Some argue that the United States was able to pull out of its worst effects in four or five years; others insist that the end did not come until the nation's urgent need for war materials in 1939–40 revived the sluggish economy. All parties agree, however, that the Great Depression of the 1930s was far more severe and widespread than all previous depressions. That depression, triggered by the stock market crash, produced monumental changes in

A COLD WIND

In The Great Depression: America in the 1930s, *T. H. Watkins clarifies the relationship between the stock market crash of 1929 and the Depression that followed:*

"When someone becomes ill after 'catching a chill,' it is not the cold itself that causes the illness. Rather the cold reduces the body's resistance to microorganisms already present in it, which then are able to cause the illness. Some such role is the proper one to assign the Crash. The cold wind that swept through lower Manhattan in October and November of 1929 lowered the economy's resistance to the point where already existing defects could multiply rapidly and bring down the whole organism."

the world, many of which are still being felt today.

PANIC IN THE BANKS

The banking industry was unable to make a quick recovery from the problems brought by the collapse of the stock market. Battered by losses from defaulted stock loans (defaulted consumer and business loans that resulted when customers lost their money in the market), and by the loss of confidence in the safety of investing money with anyone, even a bank, the nation's banks began toppling like dominoes. During 1929 there

Thousands of banks like this one in Iowa closed in the years after the stock market crash.

were only 256 bank closings reported nationwide as of November 30. That number skyrocketed to 1,352 in 1930. One of the most famous of these victims was the Bank of America, which had serviced 450,000 depositors at fifty-eight branches. Decimated when panicky customers rushed to withdraw their money, it closed its doors for good on December 11, 1930.

The pace of bank closings continued to accelerate. Nearly 2,300 banks failed in 1931, and over 5,000 shut their doors the following year. Those unlucky or trusting souls who had kept their savings in these banks generally lost most or all of their money. That meant that several more billion dollars disappeared from the economy, and millions more Americans were pushed into poverty and despair as their hard-earned life savings vanished.

AN ANCHOR ON STOCK MARKET PRICES

The expected Wall Street recovery, which might have softened some of the economic blow, never took place. The public, either because they had lost their money or their confidence, refused to reenter the market. Most stocks continued to lose value over the next three years. Even U.S. Steel, once considered among the safest and surest stocks in the world, kept sliding until it bottomed out at $138 a share, half its peak price.

The New York Stock Exchange hit its lowest point on July 8, 1932. Demand for stocks had fallen so low that only 720,000 shares traded that day, less than 5 percent of the volume recorded on that frantic October 29,

1929. Total value of the stock market shares, which had been $90 billion before the crash, bottomed out at $15.6 billion. Nearly a quarter of a century would pass before the stock market rebounded to pre-crash prices.

PRODUCTION GRINDS TO A SNAIL'S PACE

Despite optimistic forecasts by government and business officials, the nation's economy went into a tailspin that mirrored the problems on Wall Street. As savings and investment money dried up, small businesspeople and farmers found it impossible to get the loans they needed to tide them over these tough economic times. Like many banks, they could not keep their operations solvent. Over 26,000 businesses failed in 1930, more than had failed in the entire previous decade, followed by more than 28,000 failures the following year.

One result of all the bank, business, and individual failures was that the nation's large industries, already burdened by huge inventories caused by the overproduction of the 1920s, lost even more of their markets for products. This set off yet another vicious spiral of economic ruin. The less money people had, the less they could spend on products. The less money people spent on products, the harder it was for companies to stay in business. The more companies that went out of business, the fewer the people who had jobs and were earning money. The fewer people who were earning money, the less they could spend on products, and so it went.

The nation's gross national product not only declined, it nose-dived. In 1930 the United States produced 13 percent less than it had the year before. In 1931 the gross national product plummeted another 16 percent, followed by a shocking 23 percent drop the following year. By that time the nation's factory output was less than half of what it had been in the Roaring Twenties. Some crucial economic industries were even harder hit. In the early 1930s the nation's steel mills were running at only 13 percent of their capacity.

In just two years the national income of the United States dropped by one-third. Eventually it fell from a high of about $88 billion in 1929 to around $40 billion in 1932 and 1933—nearly a 60 percent drop. Farm income, which had been sluggish even in the 1920s, fell from $12 billion to $5 billion a year. Although economic experts pleaded with businesses to maintain their wages to prevent an even further erosion of consumer dollars, few could afford to do so. By 1932 factory wages had dropped more than 40 percent. The average wage earner in Oakland, California, who brought home $3,179 in 1929 was earning only $1,911 in 1933.

UNEMPLOYMENT

Even the reduced wage of the factory worker, however, would have been a blessing to the growing masses of Americans who were unable to find any way at all to earn a living. Business failures and slumping production meant that employers had no use for workers and no money to pay them. In the four years following the stock market crash, an average of one hundred thousand workers lost their jobs every week. Unemployment levels rose from just over 5 percent before the crash to 8 percent in 1930, to 15.9 percent in 1931, to 23.6 percent in 1932, and finally to a staggering 24.9 percent. That meant that one out of every four persons seeking work in the United States, a total of nearly 18 million people, could not find a job.

The situation was even worse in some urban areas. At one point during the Depression, New York City was home to nearly a million jobless. Four out of every five eligible workers in Toledo, Ohio, stood idle.

PSYCHOLOGICAL SCARS

With so many millions out of work and unable to earn income, and millions more stripped of their life's savings by the crash, the nation was ravaged by widespread

The poverty and despair that gripped Americans during the Great Depression had lasting effects on those who were forced to accept handouts in order to survive.

poverty on a scale unimaginable only a few years earlier. Families that could no longer afford house payments or rent were left with no place to live. Ghettos of makeshift, ramshackle buildings known as Hoovervilles—named after President Hoover—sprouted up around the large cities. Health standards eroded, leading to increased disease and early death. Desperate people with nothing to feed their families began to riot in the streets.

For a nation that only a few years earlier had been proclaiming a possible end to poverty in the United States, the turn of events came as a psychological shock that

During the Depression shantytowns known as Hoovervilles housed families who had lost their homes.

HAUNTING PROPHECY

Two months before he assumed the presidency, Herbert Hoover voiced a concern that turned out to be an eerily accurate prophecy, quoted in Herbert Hoover: A Public Life, *by David Burner:*

"I have no dread of the ordinary work of the presidency. What I do fear is the result of the exaggerated idea the people have conceived of me. They have a conviction that I am some sort of superman, that no problem is beyond my capacity. . . . If some unprecedented calamity should come upon the nation . . . I would be sacrificed to the unreasoning disappointment of a people who expect too much."

was to forever scar a generation. Fathers who had taken pride in working hard to provide an adequate living for their families suffered shame and in some cases loss of trust from their wives and children. Mothers floundered as they tried to cope with their loss of status and comforts of life, and tried to wring decent meals out of pitiful food budgets.

As the Depression dragged on and on, an entire younger generation began to lose hope. Elsa Ponselle, a schoolteacher from Chicago, depicted the blanket of despair under which families operated. "The Depression was a way of life for me," said Ponselle, "from the time I was twenty to the time I was thirty. I thought it was going to be forever and ever and ever. That people would always live in fear of losing their jobs. You know, fear."[32]

Even when the nation, boosted by the shot of economic adrenaline provided by the life-and-death struggle against Nazi Germany and Imperial Japan, finally did pull out of the Depression, the scars re-

mained. Psychologists documented significant psychological damage among children of the Depression, and adults found it difficult to trust the permanence of good times, the business community, or the government that they had expected to safeguard their society.

HERBERT HOOVER—HERO TO VILLAIN

Initially the main target of the public's wrath was the business community, whose excesses appeared to trigger the misery. But as the Depression dragged on with no apparent relief in sight, criticism broadened to include the federal government for not doing enough to revive the economy.

No one's reputation suffered more permanent damage from the aftershocks of the stock market crash than Herbert Hoover's. Within the span of a single term of office Hoover went from being one of the most admired presidents in over a century to the symbol of ineptness. The causes of his downfall were guilt by association, his miscalculation of the severity of the Depression, and his conviction that the government should play a limited role in business affairs.

Hoover was associated with the stock market crash and the bad economic times that followed simply because they happened during his presidency. The fact that his administration, particularly in the person of Andrew Mellon, was closely allied with business interests added to the perception that he was partially to blame.

Following the stock market crash, Hoover realized that the nation needed to revive investor and consumer confidence in the economy in order to lift it out of the spiral of despair. He attempted to do so with numerous declarations that there was nothing to worry about and that, as his vice president Charles Curtis said, "Prosperity is just around the corner."[33] In March 1930, Hoover declared that the worst was nearly over. In May he repeated much the same thing. At the end of the year he again offered an optimistic assessment of the future. But as unemployment climbed ever higher, businesses and banks failed at an accelerating rate, and poverty and misery continued to increase, those statements came back to haunt Hoover. Instead of viewing him as a leader who was trying to rally the troops, the public began to see him as a man out of touch with reality and indifferent to the fate of the masses.

That perception only increased as Hoover faithfully followed his basic belief that the government should exercise caution in its interactions with the financial world. Historically, he believed, the nation had handled depressions best by letting them work themselves out. Government interference only made matters worse. In desperate times people generally rose to the challenge and worked their way out of their own problems. But in this case the problems were far more severe than in previous economic downturns. While the government proposed limited solutions, the problems got worse, and more and more Americans fell into misery.

Hoover was not indifferent to the nation's suffering and he did attempt to take action. But his strategy was to meet with business leaders and persuade them to voluntarily take needed action, rather than impose regulations on them. For example, he extracted a commitment from Ford to raise rather than lower its wages in the early months of the Depression. He pleaded with companies not to cut back their workforces. However, few other industry leaders went along with his plans, and they quickly fell apart. Hoover was also blindsided by some business leaders, such as large banking interests, who turned on him without warning. Before the crash, they warned the federal government to stay out of all business matters. Now that they were in desperate straits, they demanded that the government step in to rescue them.

For the most part Hoover resisted such entreaties. He pushed a federal public works program through Congress to boost the nation's productivity and get people back to work. But with the federal budget pinched by drastically declining income tax revenues, little money could be found for such a program. Congress budgeted only $75 million for the program over ten years, barely a trickle in the desert of depression. The same was true of the income tax cut the Hoover administration proposed in order to stimulate the economy. The few dollars of tax relief per person would not be enough to bring the economy around, particularly as so many people had no income at all.

Still believing in the policy of laissez-faire, Hoover geared most government efforts at trying to help those plunged into poverty by the Depression rather than trying to stimulate business. His dogged belief in safeguarding individual freedom from the encroaching powers of government, which had met with enthusiastic applause in the 1920s, now became the object of scorn.

CHANGE IN PARTY ALLEGIANCE

Hoover, by now derided as a failure, was overwhelmingly defeated by Franklin Roosevelt in his bid for reelection in 1932. In some ways it was an ironic downfall. Hoover had, after all, tried to warn the nation about the dangers of excessive stock market speculation. Roosevelt, meanwhile, who was governor of New York at the time of the crash, had been one of those speculators who refused to heed the accurate warnings. Yet it was Roosevelt and the Democrats who benefited politically from the stock market crash and the Depression, in a shift that would alter the nation's political landscape for half a century.

When business leaders became objects of bitter criticism following the crash, even

The crash and the economic depression that followed caused political favor to shift to the Democratic Party. Democrat Franklin Roosevelt soundly defeated Herbert Hoover in the 1932 presidential election.

formerly popular politicians who had catered to them drew fire as well. This included Calvin Coolidge, whose popularity waned as the Depression deepened. The business-friendly policies and grudging use of government power that Republicans such as Coolidge had ridden to power during prosperous times came back to haunt them. In many people's minds the Republican Party was an accomplice to the greed of the financial community that put them in this mess. Their reluctance to use the power of government to help those in need labeled them as the party that did not care about the common people.

For most of the next half century Roosevelt's Democratic Party would reign as the majority political party in the United States. Prior to the crash, Republicans had controlled the presidency from the 1890s to 1932 with the single exception of Woodrow Wilson, who won election because of a rift in the Republican Party. After the crash, Democrats held the office for the next twenty years, and held majorities in the Congress for much of the next half century.

THE AGE OF BIG GOVERNMENT

An even more significant result of the crash and the Depression was that it ushered in the era of "big government." Prior to 1929, most people agreed that the government that governed least, governed best. They did not want the federal government, in particular, interfering in their lives.

The desperate situations in which people found themselves during the Depression, however, changed this viewpoint.

People began to believe that they needed a strong central government in Washington to protect them from the ravages of powerful, selfish business interests. Pushed into desperate economic straits by events beyond their control, and helpless to escape their plight no matter how hard they worked, they looked to the government as the only effective remedy.

As the Roosevelt administration strove to combat the grim economic situation, it enacted many emergency measures, called the New Deal, that gave the federal government a more active role in the nation's business affairs. Regulations governing the stock market were adopted. The Federal Deposit Insurance Corporation, a program in which the federal government guaranteed that depositors would get their money back should the local bank fail, was created to stabilize the banking situation. The federal government embarked on a massive public works program, spending billions of dollars on construction projects to give workers jobs and boost the economy. During the 1930s the federal government also created the Social Security system, to which workers and their employers were required to contribute, as a way to insure that all Americans would have an income in their retirement years, even if some disaster wiped out all their other assets. Assistance programs sprang up for farmers, small-business owners, disaster victims, and those mired in poverty.

The creation of federal programs has accelerated ever since then, until the federal government has grown to a size unimaginable in the 1920s. But none of these programs would have had a chance of passing

A New Era

"I have been out of touch so long with political activities that I feel I no longer fit in with these times. Great changes can come in four years. These socialistic notions of government are not of my day. When I was in office, tax reduction, tariff stability, and economy were the things to which I have paid attention. We succeeded on those lines. . . . When I read of these newfangled things that are now so popular I realize that my time in public affairs is past. I wouldn't know how to handle them if I were called upon to do so."

if not for the stock market crash and the Depression.

WORLD WAR II

Shock waves from the stock market crash rippled across the Atlantic Ocean, triggering a decade of anguish and helplessness in the Western democracies. Prior to the speculation fever that gripped the New York Stock Exchange in the late 1920s, the United States provided the financing that helped rebuild countries ravaged by World War I. Germany, in particular, desperately needed U.S. capital to help it rebuild its economy while having to pay the victorious Allies a staggering $600 million a year in war reparations. Between 1924 and 1928, Germany had borrowed more than $2 billion to stay afloat, most of it from the United States.

In 1928, however, tales of the spectacular fortunes to be made in the New York Stock Exchange caused American investors to abandon Germany and rush to the stock market. The stock market crash then sent the U.S. economy reeling so badly that its investors were in no position to return their loans to Germany. The restrictive tariff passed by the U.S. Congress worsened matters by cutting the Germans off from a major market for their nation's products. This made it impossible for them to pay off their existing loans, much less attract new sources of money. World trade slowed to a crawl.

The chain of events triggered by the U.S. stock speculation and subsequent crash threw Germany into economic chaos. Unemployment rose by two million in two months; by 1932 nearly 40 percent of all able-bodied German adults were out of work. Inflation soared out of control. Building on the

Economic fallout from the U.S. crash contributed to the rise of Nazism in Germany.

COULD IT HAPPEN AGAIN?

The effects of the stock market crash were so devastating that economic experts are frequently asked to assure the public that a similar panic and depression could never happen again. In some ways the analysts are comforting. Many safeguards have been built into the system to prevent a recurrence. The federal government has imposed rules regarding stock trading, speculation, and buying on margin. These rules are credited with helping to prevent 1987's devastating drop in the stock market from bottoming out into a 1929-like disaster. Furthermore, the federal government has stepped up to guarantee depositors' money in banks, making bank runs a thing of the past. The Federal Reserve System is responsible for regulating the economy, by manipulating interest rates and the money supply, so it does not become either too stagnant or overheated.

Nonetheless, while the experts say that a repeat of 1929 is most unlikely, they cannot rule out a similar economic disaster. There is no way to immunize U.S. society from an economic crisis that could arise from a completely unexpected chain of events. In the words of Gordon Thomas and Max Morgan-Witts, "It cannot happen again for the same reasons: Too many of Wall Street's barn doors were closed by the mass of legislation introduced as a direct result of the Crash. But only a fool would say that other circumstances could not contrive to make another crash occur."[34] After all, every reason given by economic gurus for why such a catastrophe could not take place today was uttered in the months prior to the crash of 1929.

resentments caused by the nation's unbearable economic situation, a small, radical political party known as the National Socialists, or Nazis, began attracting followers. Membership in the party doubled every six months in the years following the crash. Eventually the party's leader, Adolf Hitler, gained power, and his policies of world domination and genocide plunged the world into the most terrible war in history.

Notes

Chapter 1: The Roaring Twenties

1. Quoted in William A. Klingaman, *1929: The Year of the Great Crash*. New York: Harper & Row, 1989, p. 9.

2. Quoted in T. H. Watkins, *The Great Depression: America in the 1930s*. Boston: Little, Brown, 1993, p. 26.

3. Quoted in Gordon Thomas and Max Morgan-Witts, *The Day the Bubble Burst*. New York: Doubleday, 1979, p. 81.

4. Quoted in Tom Shachtman, *The Day America Crashed*. New York: G. P. Putnam's, 1979, p. 126.

5. Quoted in Klingaman, *1929: The Year of the Great Crash*, p. 30.

6. Lois Gordon and Alan Gordon, *American Chronicle*. New Haven: Yale University Press, 1999, p. 193.

7. Judith S. Baughman, *American Decades, 1920–29*. New York: Gale Research, 1996, p. 268.

8. Watkins, *The Great Depression: America in the 1930s*, p. 23.

9. Quoted in Gordon and Gordon, *American Chronicle*, p. 267.

10. Quoted in Gordon and Gordon, *American Chronicle*, p. 276.

Chapter 2: Growth of the Stock Market

11. Quoted in Larry Burkett, *The Coming Economic Depression*. Chicago: Moody Press, 1994, p. 33.

12. Shachtman, *The Day America Crashed*, p. 38.

13. Shachtman, *The Day America Crashed*, p. 37.

14. Quoted in Thomas and Morgan-Witts, *The Day the Bubble Burst*, p. 192.

Chapter 3: Danger Signs

15. Quoted in Thomas and Morgan-Witts, *The Day the Bubble Burst*, p. 272.

16. Quoted in Klingaman, *1929: The Year of the Great Crash*, p. 253.

17. Quoted in Thomas and Morgan-Witts, *The Day the Bubble Burst*, p. 274.

18. Baughman, *American Decades, 1920–29*, p. 103.

19. Quoted in Baughman, *American Decades, 1920–29*, p. 107.

20. Quoted in Klingaman, *1929: The Year of the Great Crash*, p. 145.

21. Quoted in Klingaman, *1929: The Year of the Great Crash*, p. 238.

Chapter 4: The Foundation Begins to Crumble

22. Quoted in Thomas and Morgan-Witts, *The Day the Bubble Burst*, p. 325.

23. Baughman, *American Decades, 1920–29*, p. 105.

24. Baughman, *American Decades, 1920–29*, p. 104.

Chapter 5: The Bottom Falls Out

25. Quoted in Shachtman, *The Day America Crashed*, p. 276.

26. Quoted in Shachtman, *The Day America Crashed*, p. 280.

27. Quoted in Baughman, *American Decades, 1920–29*, p. 106.

Chapter 6: Immediate Effect of the Crash on Americans

28. Quoted in Thomas and Morgan-Witts, *The Day the Bubble Burst*, p. xv.

29. Baughman, *American Decades, 1920–29*, p. 106.

30. Quoted in Lois Gordon and Alan Gordon, *The Columbia Chronicles of American Life, 1910–1992*. New York: Columbia University Press, 1995, p. 195.

31. Shachtman, *The Day America Crashed*, p. 248.

Chapter 7: Long-Term Effects of the Stock Market Crash

32. Quoted in Watkins, *The Great Depression: America in the 1930s*, p. 13.

33. Quoted in David Burner, *Herbert Hoover: A Public Life*. New York: Knopf, 1979, p. 250.

34. Thomas and Morgan-Witts, *The Day the Bubble Burst*, p. 425.

For Further Reading

Kathleen Brenna, *Stock Market Crash of 1929.* New York: Chelsea House, 2000. One of the recent overviews of the events of 1929.

Barbara Silberbick Feinberg, *Black Tuesday: The Stock Market Crash of 1929.* Brookfield, CT: Millbrook, 1995. A discussion of the crash, the Depression that followed, and the attempts to combat it.

Nancy Millichap, *The Stock Market Crash of 1929.* New York: Silver-Burdett, 1994. A somewhat shorter version of the events that led to the crash and the Great Depression, and steps taken to prevent a recurrence.

Works Consulted

Books

Judith S. Baughman, *American Decades, 1920–29*. New York: Gale Research, 1996. A year-by-year survey of political, social, and scientific events of the 1920s.

Larry Burkett, *The Coming Economic Depression*. Chicago: Moody Press, 1994. The author presents his perspective on the events that precipitated the Great Depression as background to his predictions for the future of the economy.

David Burner, *Herbert Hoover: A Public Life*. New York: Knopf, 1979. Thorough coverage of one of the most misunderstood presidents.

Carol Gelderman, *Henry Ford: The Wayward Capitalist*. New York: Dial Press, 1981. As an anti–Wall Street, big-business tycoon, Ford offers a unique perspective on the crash.

Lois Gordon and Alan Gordon, *American Chronicle*. New Haven: Yale University Press, 1999. Slices of life from the American experience.

———, *The Columbia Chronicles of American Life, 1910–1992*. New York: Columbia University Press, 1995. More of the same as described above, with numerous quotes, statistics, and photos.

James Grant, *Bernard Baruch: The Adventures of a Wall Street Legend*. New York: Simon & Schuster, 1987. Perspective of the crash from the vantage point of a cautious investor.

William A. Klingaman, *1929: The Year of the Great Crash*. New York: Harper & Row, 1989. A thorough treatment of the events leading up to the crash with numerous anecdotes and stories of those affected.

Ted Morgan, *FDR: A Biography*. New York: Simon & Schuster, 1985. This large biography presents Roosevelt's view of the crash and onslaught of the Depression.

Tom Shachtman, *The Day America Crashed*. New York: G. P. Putnam's, 1979. A very readable and understandable analysis of the events surrounding the October 1929 crash.

Robert Sobel, *Coolidge: An American Enigma*. Washington, DC: Regnery Publishers, 1998. Short, readable book that tries to delve into the life of the taciturn man who presided over the prosperity and excesses of the 1920s.

Jean Strouse, *Morgan: American Financier*. New York: Random House, 1999.

Gordon Thomas and Max Morgan-Witts, *The Day the Bubble Burst*. New York: Doubleday, 1979. Fascinating book that focuses on October 24, not the traditional Black Tuesday, October 29, as the day that the foundations of Wall Street were shaken to their core.

T. H. Watkins, *The Great Depression: America in the 1930s*. Boston: Little, Brown, 1993. Focuses on life after the crash, with emphasis on individual stories.

———, *The Hungry Years*. New York: Henry Holt, 1995. Similar to above.

Bernard Weisberger, *The Dream Maker: William C. Durant, Founder of GM*. Boston: Little, Brown, 1979. Life story of perhaps the biggest gambler the stock market has ever known.

Periodicals

Douglas Dozier, "Bootleg Loans," *Atlantic Monthly*, June 1929.

Index

Picture Credits

Cover Photo: Library of Congress

Archive Photos, 13, 46

Archive Photos/American Stock, 14

Archive Photos/Hulton Getty, 9

Archive/Popperphoto, 41

Corbis/Bettmann, 22, 30, 32, 36, 56, 59, 65, 67, 80, 82, 90

Corbis, 52, 61

Corbis/Purcell Team, 29

Corbis/Underwood & Underwood, 53

FPG Intl., 11, 20, 25, 42, 44, 47, 58, 63, 71, 75, 77, 93

FPG Intl./National Archives, 89

Library of Congress, 96

Stock Montage, 17, 39, 70, 73, 86

About the Author

Nathan Aaseng is the author of more than 150 books for young readers on a variety of subjects including *The Cougar, Women Olympic Champions*, and *The White House* for Lucent Books. Aaseng, from Eau Claire, Wisconsin, was the 1999 recipient of the Wisconsin Library Association's Notable Wisconsin Author Award.